COMPOSITION SKILLS ACTIVITIES KIT

Ready-to-Use Lessons and Exercises for Grades 7–12

Phil Schlemmer and Dori Schlemmer

Illustrated by Kate Diedrich

THE CENTER FOR APPLIED RESEARCH IN EDUCATION
West Nyack, New York 10995

10 9 8 7 6 5 4 3 2 1

Printed in the United States of America

Library of Congress Cataloging-in-Publication Data

Schlemmer, Phil.
    Composition skills activities kit: ready-to-use lessons and
exercises for grades 7-12 / Phil Schlemmer and Dori Schlemmer;
illustrated by Kate Diedrich.
      p.   cm.
    ISBN 0-87628-244-3
    1. Composition (Language arts)   2. English language--Rhetoric.
I. Schlemmer, Dori. II. Title.
LB1631.S2645 1989
808′.042′0712--dc20
                                                        89-36231
                                                           CIP

ISBN 0-87628-244-3

**THE CENTER FOR APPLIED
RESEARCH IN EDUCATION**
BUSINESS & PROFESSIONAL DIVISION
A division of Simon & Schuster
West Nyack, New York 10995

About the Authors

Phil Schlemmer, M.Ed., has been designing and teaching skill-oriented activities since 1973, when he began his master's program in alternative education at Indiana University. From 1973 to 1985 he helped create a full-time school in Grand Rapids, Michigan, for motivated sixth graders, with one year out as the director of a magnet high school. Mr. Schlemmer has since been teaching and conducting teacher workshops in the Holland, Michigan, Public Schools. His workshops show how to prepare students for learning by teaching them research, presentation, and higher-level thinking skills.

Dori Schlemmer assists her husband in the development, documentation, writing, and publication of educational materials. She is a former teacher and an accomplished photographer who devoted much time to help write, rewrite, edit, and revise the five-book set of classroom activities by Phil Schlemmer, *Learning on Your Own* (Center for Applied Research in Education, 1987). She is actively involved in developing new ideas for her husband's workshops and for future publishing efforts.

About This Resource

The purpose of the *Composition Skills Activities Kit* is to provide structured, sequenced lessons that help your students think about issues critically, express ideas creatively, state opinions clearly, or present information concisely. The reading material is designed to explain why critical, creative, clear, concise writing is desirable. During each activity, students will:

- formulate opinions
- explore topics of interest
- express original ideas
- conduct research
- practice the use of basic writing skills
- produce a final written product

The twenty-five activities in the *Composition Skills Activities Kit* are designed for use in secondary classes, grades 7–12; their difficulty increases as you advance through the book. Each activity follows the same format, providing a Teacher Preview and four fully-developed, reproducible lessons:

Introductory Narrative: This is a short, first-person narrative written in the voice of a student who has realized, through a personal experience, that writing can be a valuable skill. This narrator is a fictional character invented by the authors.

Reading Material: This is a longer piece of written material that is directly related to the Introductory Narrative. It may be something written by the same fictional student, to serve as a model for students to follow, or it may be an informational piece that provides facts or instructions needed for future assignments. In either case, the Reading Material leads right into the classroom and independent assignments.

Classroom Assignment: This is an assignment sheet for a lesson that normally requires one or two class sessions. Most Classroom Assignments involve brainstorming, class discussions, and brief writing or research activities; they usually set the stage for independent writing in On Your Own.

On Your Own: This is the assignment for an independent writing project. Each project is unique, but every one helps to build the thinking process of the writer in some way. Assignments range from making informative posters to writing speeches to composing fictional character descriptions to producing formal research papers. Refer to the Teacher Preview Chart for a complete synopsis of each activity's lessons.

Most of the activities cover very general subject areas, such as research, current events, literature, history, science, and so forth; some are not subject-specific at all. Decisions about particular subject matter are left up to you, and students are encouraged to choose their own topics, often from lists developed during class discussions. For example, Activity 14, "Writing a Biography," can be used to have students write about European monarchies, Chinese dynasties, New World explorers, Renaissance artists, American writers, World War II heroes, and so on. Students choose their own topics from within the specified subject area, thereby incorporating a personalized writing project into the curriculum.

Writing has long been considered the most powerful and enduring form of communication; the ability to write intelligently and creatively is a key to success in the modern world. Unfortunately, the importance of the written word is often underestimated in an age of computers, televisions, and word processors. One of the challenges a teacher must face head-on is the problem of motivating students and making writing assignments that are "relevant." This book is designed to help you build such assignments into your classes.

Phil Schlemmer
Dori Schlemmer

Contents

Activity 20. Preparing a Résumé • 147

Activity 21. Producing an Oral Presentation • 153

Activity 22. Studying Current Issues • 161

Activity 23. Writing About Your World • 168

Activity 24. Learning to Learn • 177

Activity 25. Writing a Research Paper • 184

TEACHER PREVIEW CHART

(Activities 1–8)

TEACHER PREVIEW	APPLICATION	INTRODUCTORY NARRATIVE
Activity 1	Finding Answers to Questions	"Up, Up, and Away"—Denise becomes interested in hot air balloons after seeing one; then she develops a mini-lesson about how they work.
Activity 2	Making and Using Posters	"Fun at the Fireworks"—Randy tells about getting ready to see the fireworks after seeing them advertised in a poster display.
Activity 3	Using the Card Catalog	"Looking for Facts"—Jerome explains how he made use of his knowledge of the card catalog to learn about his favorite subject: rockets.
Activity 4	Making Use of Your Time	"Time's a-Wastin'"—Anne tells how a challenge from her mother made her think about wasting time and making better use of it.
Activity 5	Creating a Script	"The Show Must Go On"—Kim explains why she and her friends decided to produce a "Summer Playhouse" in her backyard.
Activity 6	Writing a Business Letter	"Sincerely Yours"—Felicia tells why she had to learn how to write a business letter to apply for a grant.
Activity 7	Composing a Speech	"Good Evening, Ladies and Gentlemen"—Ben explains why he made a speech to the local school board about the fate of a piece of property the board wants to sell.
Activity 8	Interviewing an Adult	"May I Ask a Few Questions?"—Julie describes her interest in journalism and explains why she decided to interview her grandmother.

READING MATERIAL	CLASSROOM ASSIGNMENT	ON YOUR OWN
Denise's mini-lesson, written for fourth or fifth grade students.	Write an answer for younger students to a question taken from a recently completed unit of study.	Choose a question from a list and use at least one reference book to write an answer for younger students.
A poster advertising a "Fireworks Festival."	Record facts from the poster, then write a radio advertisement for the Fireworks Festival.	Produce a poster about a personally chosen local or school event.
A description of the Dewey decimal classification system and examples of cards from the card catalog.	Answer questions about the catalog cards from the Reading Material	Choose a topic from a list and go to a library to find reference information from the card catalog.
Anne's "Daily Agenda" chart and an excerpt from her journal.	Discuss what a typical student's daily agenda might look like, then work on a personal agenda.	Work on a promotional campaign to change how people spend their time by writing an advertisement and making a pamphlet.
Kim's play script, titled "The Trial."	Develop an introduction to a play.	Write a one-act play.
Basic information about business letters, followed by examples.	Write a business letter based on one of four scenarios supplied on the assignment sheet.	Write a scenario that would require an exchange of business letters, then write the letters.
Basic information about speechmaking, followed by the outline and text of Ben's speech.	List topics about which speeches could be made, then choose one topic and record several points that should be emphasized.	Outline a speech about the topic chosen for the Classroom Assignment; then compose a final written version.
An introduction to interviewing, followed by a transcript of Julie's interview.	Interview a guest speaker in a press conference format, then write a summary from notes.	Conduct an interview with an adult and write a transcript or summary of it.

TEACHER PREVIEW CHART

(Activities 9–15)

TEACHER PREVIEW	APPLICATION	INTRODUCTORY NARRATIVE
Activity 9	Recording Information on Notecards	"Bits and Pieces"—Anthony tells about learning to conduct a research project by recording facts on notecards.
Activity 10	Describing a News Event	"Tell It Like It Is"—John explains how he botched an effort to write an article, and he offers a clearly written revision.
Activity 11	Reading for Pleasure	"The Choice Is Yours"—Lisa describes her successful attempt to convince her English teacher to bring more contemporary readings into the literature class curriculum.
Activity 12	Writing for Pleasure	"A Ticket to Write"—José tells about a writing course he is taking and why he is enjoying it.
Activity 13	Getting to the Point	"Don't Beat Around the Bush"—Rick explains why he admires people who are frank and straightforward, then he describes a personal situation where frankness would have helped.
Activity 14	Writing a Biography	"A Real-Life Story"—Angela relates how she became interested in Alexander the Great, and she explains how she came to write his biography.
Activity 15	Describing Characters	"Words of a Master: Charles Dickens"—Caleb describes how he became interested in reading Charles Dickens' stories after being assigned to find examples of character descriptions by famous authors.

READING MATERIAL	CLASSROOM ASSIGNMENT	ON YOUR OWN
Information about making notecards and bibliographies, followed by samples of Anthony's work.	Conduct an "information search" to find facts about specific topics; record them on notecards.	Choose a topic from a list, conduct research, record facts on notecards, prepare a bibliography, and write a short report.
Suggestions for being a good journalistic writer, followed by John's original, poorly written article.	View a 10-minute video, then list the sequence of action. Meet in a small group to compare notes.	Collect information about a current event topic, keep a scrapbook/journal of clippings and notes, then write a summary article.
A definition of an annotated bibliography, followed by bibliographic information about the books listed in the "Young Adults' Choices."	Study the "Young Adults' Choices" bibliography, choose three titles that are interesting, and explain in writing why they are appealing.	Choose a book to read and write an annotated bibliography for it.
José's paper titled "Why I Like to Write Short Stories."	Discuss and list the various types of writing people do. Choose a personal favorite and explain why in a paper.	Create an example of your favorite type of writing.
Rick's letter to his friend, Steven, in which he unsuccessfully tries to offer constructive criticism of a science project.	Outline the points that Rick really meant to make to Steven, then rewrite his letter.	Choose a situation from the assignment sheet; write a letter, as if to a friend, expressing personal opinions and advice.
Angela's biography of Alexander the Great.	From within a specified subject area, identify people about whom biographies could be written, and verify that information is available.	Choose a name from the class list, locate sources of information, prepare a bibliography, and write a short biography.
Character descriptions from Charles Dickens' *Pickwick Papers*.	Rewrite one of Dickens' character descriptions using more contemporary language.	Write a detailed character description as if it were being developed for a short story or novel.

TEACHER PREVIEW CHART

(Activities 16–23)

TEACHER PREVIEW	APPLICATION	INTRODUCTORY NARRATIVE
Activity 16	Presenting Information Visually	"A Poster's Worth a Thousand Words"—Paul tells how he learned about the value of visual aids when he had to present information to a class of fifth graders.
Activity 17	Charting Data	"The Numbers Game"—Susan describes a science assignment that required her to organize and chart data.
Activity 18	Expressing Ideas in an Editorial	"In My Opinion"—Cara explains how, as school newspaper editor, she had to deal with a freedom of the press issue.
Activity 19	Describing Action	"Words of a Master: Stephen Crane"—Joshua tells about his introduction to Stephen Crane's work and how that discovery led him to try his hand at describing action.
Activity 20	Preparing a Résumé	"You Are What You Write"—Russell tells about trying to get a work-study job and being rejected because of an improperly prepared résumé.
Activity 21	Producing an Oral Presentation	"A Picture and a Thousand Words"—Erin describes a camera club activity that required an oral presentation to be given at a photography exhibit.
Activity 22	Studying Current Issues	"As the World Turns"—John explains how a project in his history class helped him realize the importance of understanding events in the modern world.
Activity 23	Writing About Your World	"For Future Reference"—Jason tells about using an old newspaper as a reference for a research project that gives his teacher a new project idea.

READING MATERIAL	CLASSROOM ASSIGNMENT	ON YOUR OWN
An information sheet with procedures and hints for making a quality poster.	Use the facts that are provided to design a poster that Paul could have used in his presentation.	Choose a topic from an assigned subject area; design and produce an attractive, informative poster.
The data sheet given to Susan by her teacher containing unorganized facts about four unrelated topics.	Categorize the facts on the data sheet. Choose one category and graph or chart all the available data.	Choose a topic, collect data through research, and produce a visual presentation of the information.
Cara's editorial about freedom of speech in the school paper.	Search for editorials in materials provided in class. Choose one, underline important ideas, and summarize the central idea.	Choose a topic and outline ideas for an editorial. Upon receiving approval, write the editorial.
An explanation of writing in the "active voice," followed by excerpts from *The Red Badge of Courage*.	Choose a situation from a list and write a one-paragraph description of the action that might take place.	Choose a situation from a list and write a two-page (minimum) description of the action that might take place.
Suggestions for writing a good résumé, followed by two examples: one improperly and the other properly done.	Using information that is provided, write a résumé for a person who is applying for a job at an imaginary company.	Write your own personal résumé.
An information sheet about making oral presentations.	Develop materials that will help younger students make oral presentations.	Choose a topic and prepare an oral presentation. One ten-minute presentation will be given each day for six weeks.
An article about teaching current events in secondary schools.	In a small group, choose a current event and collect articles and clippings for a scrapbook or collage. (Three-day activity)	Choose a current event to follow for a period of time. Write a summary of each week's happenings in a journal.
Jason's paper about the events of one day, as seen through the eyes of a seventeen-year old in 1968.	Pretending to be a journalist in the year 2025, collect information from magazines and newspapers about life in the 1990s.	Write an essay about the present that would help describe the 1990s to a person in the year 2025.

TEACHER PREVIEW CHART

(Activities 24–25)

TEACHER PREVIEW	APPLICATION	INTRODUCTORY NARRATIVE
Activity 24	Learning to Learn	"Digging Deeper"—Amanda explains how she became interested in whales and marine biology following a brief discussion in her biology class.
Activity 25	Writing a Research Paper	"Just the Facts, Please"—Linda explains why she had to learn how to compose a research paper so she could apply for a job at the zoo.

READING MATERIAL	CLASSROOM ASSIGNMENT	ON YOUR OWN
A paper written by Amanda about becoming a marine biologist and studying whales.	Write about a career choice if it had to be made today. What factors influenced this choice?	Write an essay that is an endorsement of a specific job or occupational field, encouraging someone to give it consideration.
General guidelines for preparing a research paper, followed by Linda's report on orang-utans.	Discuss the use of footnotes and their proper form, then write footnotes for various books and magazines.	Choose a topic and prepare a "working bibliography" that could serve as the beginning of a research report project.

ACTIVITY 1.
Finding Answers to Questions

TEACHER PREVIEW

LESSON DESCRIPTIONS

Introductory Narrative ("Up, Up, and Away"): Denise describes the first time she saw a hot air balloon, and she explains how her interest in hot air balloons helped her complete a writing assignment in her English class.

Reading Material: Denise's mini-lesson, "How Does a Hot Air Balloon Work?" which was written as instructional material for students in the fourth or fifth grade.

Classroom Assignment: Students write answers to a question that you provide at the beginning of the class period. Choose a topic that everyone in the class should know about (taken from a recently completed unit of study), and write a question that each person should be able to answer. For example, if the Babylonian Empire has just been covered in history, a question such as "What is the Code of Hammurabi?" could be asked. Allowing students to use their history textbooks for reference, instruct them to write brief answers to the question. The answers should be written so that younger students can learn from them. When they are finished, have students read and discuss their papers in class. Place emphasis on clear, concise, simple writing.

On Your Own: Each student chooses a question from a list of thirty that is provided on the assignment sheet. The question is to be answered in two or three paragraphs, using at least one reference book for information. The goal is to produce a mini-lesson that could be used with a fourth or fifth grade class. Students are also given the option of writing answers to their own questions, but the questions must receive your approval first.

An alternate approach is to put notecards numbered one through thirty in a box and have each student draw one. This becomes his or her question to answer. For example, the student drawing card 10 would write a brief explanation of why leaves are green. Remember, this requires some research.

1

SUGGESTIONS FOR SETTING THE STAGE

- Come to class with a set of questions and ask students where they would find answers to them. Discuss common, everyday situations when people need to find answers to questions. Here is a sample list of questions. Add more if you wish.

  - Is my favorite television show on tonight?
  - Did the Tigers win their ball game yesterday?
  - How many people live in our town/city?
  - How do you prepare chicken cacciatore?
  - Who was the fortieth president of the United States?
  - How much does a record album cost?
  - What will the weather be like tomorrow?
  - How does acid rain affect us?
  - What kinds of jobs are available in our town?
  - What classes should I take in high school?

  During the discussion of these questions, emphasize the importance of being able to find answers to your own questions.

- Come to class with pictures, models, films, or demonstrations of hot air balloons and how they work. Introduce students to the activity by initiating a discussion of balloons.

Name _____ Date _____

INTRODUCTORY NARRATIVE

Read the following narrative to find out how Denise used her interest in hot air balloons to complete a writing assignment for her English teacher.

Up, Up, and Away
by Denise

I became interested in hot air balloons the first time I saw one three years ago. I was riding my bike down the street when I heard a heavy hissing sound above me in the sky. It sounded like a dragon breathing fire out of its mouth. I stopped by the side of the street and got off my bike to see what was up there. Of course it wasn't a dragon, but it *was* something I'd never seen: a huge, brightly colored balloon, hanging almost motionless in the sky above me. I could see a couple of tiny people in the basket so I waved and they waved back. Then I saw a flame shoot from the basket up into the balloon, and I heard the dragon-like noise again. The balloon rose up higher and slowly drifted out of sight past the woods.

Balloons have been my hobby ever since that day. I have posters, models, photographs, postcards, and books. I even got to ride in a balloon last summer when my dad hired a man to take us up for my birthday. What a present! Anyway, it should not be surprising that, when a recent English assignment allowed me to write about balloons, I was very pleased. It gave me a chance to write about something in which I have a strong interest.

My English teacher, Mrs. Peters, teaches a unit called "Finding Answers to Questions," which emphasizes research and writing. For one of our projects she gave the class a list of questions and we each selected one to work with. Our assignment was to find information and write an answer that could be used to help teach fourth or fifth grade students. In other words, we were asked to produce a mini-lesson of two or three paragraphs that answered a specific question. The question I chose was: How does a hot air balloon work?

I enjoyed this assignment. It was a challenge to write for younger students because I had to be simple, clear, and to the point. You really have to understand something in order to explain it to others, especially in writing. I think I did a pretty good job, too. Any fourth grader who wants to know more about hot air balloons could read my lesson and learn a lot.

Name _____   Date _____

READING MATERIAL

Writing instructional materials for younger students is an excellent way to improve your ability to state facts and information in an understandable way. This type of activity helps you learn to write simply and clearly.

 Read Denise's lesson on hot air balloons below. As you read, notice that she included quite a bit of information without using big words, difficult concepts, or complex sentences. She knew she was writing to an audience of fourth or fifth graders, and she used a style that fit her readers.

How Does a Hot Air Balloon Work?
by Denise

People have been flying in balloons for over 200 years. Even though balloons made these days are much safer and easier to fly than balloons made in the past, their basic design is the same. Each is made up of a gas (or air) bag, a car which hangs below the gas bag, a heat source, and a valve system so the pilot can let air out.

 Hot air balloons work because hot air is lighter than cool air. When the air inside the gas bag is heated, the balloon will rise off the ground. The more it is heated, the faster it will rise. A propane burner heats the gas. It is mounted on a metal frame between the gas bag and the car. The pilot turns on the burner during takeoff and whenever he or she wants the balloon to rise higher during the trip. When the balloon reaches a certain height above the ground, the burner is turned off and the balloon drifts silently in air currents. The best and safest time to take off in a hot air balloon is just after sunrise or a few hours before sunset. This is when the air is the calmest.

 When it's time to land, the pilot looks for a flat, clear area where the balloon can touch down without getting caught or torn on anything. Air is let out of the gas bag a little at a time through a valve so that the balloon lands slowly and gently. Once the car touches ground the pilot pulls a rip cord which opens a large panel in the top of the balloon. This lets the air out quickly, and the air bag loses its lifting power.

 Before someone may pilot a hot air balloon it is necessary to take lessons, pass tests, and get a pilot certificate. A person must be at least fourteen years old to become a certified balloon pilot, but anyone can be a passenger.

BIBLIOGRAPHY

HAYMAN, LEROY. *All About Balloons, Blimps and Dirigibles.* New York: Julian Messner, 1980.
KIRSCHNER, EDWIN J. *Aerospace Balloons.* California: Aero Publishers, Inc., 1985.

Name _____   Date _____

CLASSROOM ASSIGNMENT

In the space below, write an answer to a question that your teacher will provide in class. The answer to the question can be found in one of your textbooks. Your assignment is to find the proper information and rewrite it so that a fourth or fifth grade student could understand it. Be prepared to read your answer to the class.

Record the question here: _____

_____

_____

Record your answer here and continue on the back if necessary:

_____

_____

_____

_____

_____

_____

_____

_____

_____

_____

_____

_____

_____

Name _____ **Date** _____

ON YOUR OWN

Prepare a two- or three-paragraph answer to one of the questions below. Organize the answer as if you were writing a mini-lesson for a younger student, someone in the fourth or fifth grade. Be *sure* all of your facts are correct! Locate at least one reference book to use as a source of information, and include a bibliography with your answer.

Question: _____

_____

Due date: _____

Questions

1. How long ago did dinosaurs live on earth?
2. How big do whales get?
3. What does "internal combustion engine" mean?
4. How powerful is lightning?
5. What is acid rain?
6. How does a jet engine work?
7. What did Neil Armstrong do?
8. What is a wallaby?
9. How is maple syrup made?
10. Why are leaves green?
11. When and how did Israel become a country?
12. What is the stock market?
13. What was the "gold rush?"
14. What was the "Apollo" space project?
15. How big is the earth?
16. Why is the sky blue?
17. What is a rainbow?
18. What causes wind?
19. What was the "Great Depression?"
20. How did World War II start?
21. Where and why was the first atomic bomb built?
22. What is a glacier?
23. What is a hybrid plant or animal?
24. What are stalagmites and stalactites?
25. What is a comet?
26. Where and why was the first shot fired in the Revolutionary War?
27. What is the electoral college?
28. How does a tornado form?
29. What are "simple machines?"
30. How big and hot is the sun?
31. You may write about a question of your own with teacher approval. Record your question below.

_____

_____

_____ approved   _____ not approved

Comments:

ACTIVITY 2.
Making and Using Posters

TEACHER PREVIEW

LESSON DESCRIPTIONS:

Introductory Narrative ("Fun at the Fireworks"): Randy tells about getting ready to go see the fireworks after seeing them advertised in a poster display.

Reading Material: A poster advertising a fireworks festival.

Classroom Assignment: Students record facts from the Fireworks Festival poster, then write a one paragraph advertisement for the festival that could be read on radio.

On Your Own. Students produce their own posters about local or school events.

SUGGESTIONS FOR SETTING THE STAGE:

- Bring a film or video tape of a fireworks display to class. The one hundredth birthday of the Statue of Liberty offers a well-documented possibility. Tell students they will be writing a radio advertisement for a fireworks display, and to think of creative ways to present their advertisement as they watch the film.

- Bring a selection of posters to class. These can be collected from around town as they become outdated. Student-made posters can also be used. Critically analyze each poster with the class by discussing its effectiveness in advertising whatever event or product it displays.

- Give everyone a piece of 12″ × 18″ art paper, then describe a local or school event. Give all the important details by outlining them on the board, and ask each student to design a poster for it. This should be a rough draft, done in pencil, that shows where information will be located and what kinds of headings, slogans, and illustrations will be included. However, "rough" does not mean sloppy, and neatness should be emphasized. If you wish, final drafts can be made.

Name _____ Date _____

INTRODUCTORY NARRATIVE

Read the following narrative to find out how Randy made use of an advertising poster to help him plan his family's next trip to a fireworks display.

Fun at the Fireworks
by Randy

Yesterday afternoon, on my way home from school, I decided to walk to the post office and pick up the latest commemorative stamp that had just been released for sale. I've been a stamp collector ever since I was five years old. I have over 1,000 interesting stamps from countries all around the world.

As I came out of the post office and strolled home along Main Street, a poster in a hardware window caught my eye. I could see the words "Fireworks Festival" written across the top in big letters, so I crossed the street to get a better look.

Ever since I can remember I've loved going to see fireworks. Each year my family packs a big blanket, a thermos full of lemonade, and some snacks in my dad's duffle bag. We go early enough to get a good spot; then we have a party until it gets dark. My younger brother usually tries to scare us by making weird noises and holding a flashlight under his face so that he looks like Frankenstein's monster.

Since I planned to invite a friend to go with us to see the fireworks this year, I needed to find out what day they will be displayed and if they'll be on the east side of town by the bay. There's a great pizza place three blocks from the water called "Big Al's Sizzlin' Pizza" where we can go to eat afterward.

The poster told me everything I needed to know, so I went home and called my friend right away to make plans for the fireworks. He said that he could go, and I'm really looking forward to it.

Name _____   Date _____

READING MATERIAL

Even though reading a poster is easier than reading a page out of a book, it serves an important purpose. Posters provide information about current events in the community. Since the reader doesn't usually have paper and pen to write down facts, the poster should highlight important details and present them visually in such a way that they will be remembered.

Read the poster below carefully. Notice how it was made to look attractive:

- Big letters for important words
- Straight lines of well-spaced letters
- A drawing of a fireworks display
- A neat border

Can you understand the information? Should more facts be provided? Are there any misspelled words? Sometimes posters look messy, have writing mistakes, or are confusing. Posters should be simple and easy to read, and it takes planning and patience to make a good one.

FIREWORKS FESTIVAL

Friday, October 12
At Seaside Park

HELP OUR CITY CELEBRATE ITS SESQUICENTENNIAL

Festival events include:

1. Clowns, jugglers and mime artists (7:00–8:00 P.M.)
2. Modern Symphony concert at the band shell (8:00–9:00 P.M.)
3. Food booths serving refreshments at the pavilion from 6:00–9:00 P.M.
4. Fireworks at 9:00 P.M. (just after dark)

City ordinances prohibit the use of alcoholic beverages in the park.

Name ————————————————   Date ————————————————

CLASSROOM ASSIGNMENT

I. Study the Fireworks Festival poster to find answers for the following questions. Notice what kinds of facts are important to include on a poster about an event such as a fireworks display.

LOCATION: Where will the fireworks be held? ——————————————————

DATE: What day of the month will they be displayed? ——————————————

TIME: What time will they start? ————————————————————————

REFRESHMENTS: Where will food be available in the park? ————————————

RULES: Is alcohol allowed in the park? ————————————————————

REASON FOR EVENT: What is the city celebrating? ——————————————

MUSIC: What music group will be performing? ————————————————

ENTERTAINMENT: Who will perform between 7:00 and 8:00 PM? ——————————

II. Write a one- or two-paragraph radio advertisement for the Fireworks Festival. Include all the important details. You may be as creative as you wish with your advertisement, but it must be a positive, effective effort to get people to come to the Festival. The listener should clearly understand what, when, where, why, and so forth. Be prepared to read your radio advertisement if called upon.

——————————————————————————————————————

——————————————————————————————————————

——————————————————————————————————————

——————————————————————————————————————

——————————————————————————————————————

——————————————————————————————————————

——————————————————————————————————————

——————————————————————————————————————

Name _____ **Date** _____

ON YOUR OWN

Create a poster about something that is going to happen in your town, neighborhood, or school. Include at least six facts about the event that you think are important. Before working on the final poster, plan and sketch a "practice" poster on a piece of typewriter or art paper. You can also use the boxes below to play with the "look" of your poster.

Decide on:

- a main heading or title
- a way of stating each fact so it is clear and concise
- a simple design, drawing, or picture that attracts attention
- the arrangement of facts and art on the poster

Hints for making a quality poster:

- Be sure all words are spelled correctly.
- Use large letters for the main headings.
- Print information on straight lines which have been drawn *lightly* in pencil and can be erased later.
- Use bright easy to read colors.
- Leave a border around the edge.

ACTIVITY 3.
Using the Card Catalog

TEACHER PREVIEW

LESSON DESCRIPTIONS

Introductory Narrative ("Looking for Facts"): Jerome explains how he made use of his knowledge of the card catalog to learn about his favorite subject, rockets.

Reading Material: A brief description of the Dewey decimal classification system, and copies of the cards Jerome found in the catalog.

Classroom Assignment: Students answer questions about information from the cards in the reading material.

On Your Own: Students choose topics from a list and go to a library to find book call numbers, authors, and titles in the card catalog.

SUGGESTIONS FOR SETTING THE STAGE

- Bring poster-size examples of subject, author, and title catalog cards to class to initiate a discussion about the value or usefulness of a card catalog in a library. Tell students they are college history majors working on a final research paper. Of what importance is the catalog to a person doing such work? Be creative thinkers: come up with as many ideas as possible. Here are some suggestions:

  - It "indexes" the library, making the collection accessible.
  - It categorizes areas of knowledge and puts them into sections of the library.
  - It allows a person to "browse" through the library without leaving his or her seat.
  - It places all of the titles by a single author together.
  - It places all of the titles about a single topic together.
  - It tells if the library has a particular book.
  - Each card contains valuable information:

    * a brief synopsis (Is this a book I want?)

   * publication date (How old is the book?)

   * a number to locate the book in the library (Where do I find it?)

   * keys to other places to look in the catalog (What else is available?)

   * the author (Is this someone I've heard of? If it's a good book, are there more by the same author?)

   * illustrations, maps, photographs, and so forth (Can I learn by looking as well as by reading?)

• Describe a scenario in which a student must find some books. Give the class five minutes to record each step a person would have to take to locate the books in the library, for example:

   – a book by John F. Kennedy; the last word of the title is "Courage".

   – a book entitled *Moby Dick*.

   – a book about growing your own herbs and spices.

   – any book by Isaac Asimov.

TEACHER ANSWERS: (CLASSROOM ASSIGNMENT)

1. 600–699 (technology or applied sciences)
2. *The Complete Encyclopedia of Space Satellites* (1986)
3. *Missiles and Rockets* (1975)
4. *The Rocket's Red Glare,* Wernher von Braun and Frederick I. Ordway III
5. *The Rocket's Red Glare*—author
   Handbook of Model Rocketry—title
   Complete Encyclopedia of Space Satellites—subject
   Missiles and Rockets—subject
   An Illustrated History of Space Shuttle—subject
6. *Handbook of Model Rocketry*
7. The book is illustrated.
8. A list of sources that the author used to help write the book.
9. The first one or two letters of the author's name.
10.

8	2	4	1
3	9	7	
10	5	6	

Name _____   Date _____

INTRODUCTORY NARRATIVE

Read the following narrative to find out how Jerome's interest in rockets led him to make use of his knowledge of the card catalog at the public library.

Looking for Facts
by Jerome

I'm not sure exactly when I became interested in rockets and space travel; my dad says it was the day I was born. He's only kidding, but I *have* been fascinated with outer space for most of my life. At first I just talked about being an astronaut and dreamed of having fun while floating around in weightlessness, but recently I've decided to learn everything I can about rockets and how they work. I want to be a space scientist when I grow up.

When my interest in rockets became serious, I realized that I had to find information on my own, and the logical place to start was the local public library. The library skills I learned in school suddenly became valuable as I began my independent study, and I was thankful for my knowledge of the card catalog. I knew that I could look up "rockets" and find some books, but I also had the title of one book I wanted to find—*Handbook of Model Rocketry*—and my science teacher advised me to look up some titles by Wernher von Braun.

The first trip to the library was very productive. I located eight books by Wernher von Braun, and I checked out *The Rocket's Red Glare*. I found a title card for *Handbook of Model Rocketry* which led me right to that book, and I found three other excellent sources of information in the catalog under "rockets." My understanding of the Dewey decimal classification system and knowledge of the arrangement of the library allowed me to quickly locate the books. Since I have my own library card, I was soon headed home with a mini-library on rocketry in my backpack. My time spent browsing through the card catalog showed me that there are also books available about people, history, mathematics, and other topics related to rocketry that I can check out in the future. Having access to information like this is great; it makes my hobby of learning about rockets a lot easier and a lot more fun!

Name _____   Date _____

READING MATERIAL

The card (or computer) catalog is the most important reference resource in the library. Without a catalog, it would be impossible to find the books you want. But even with a catalog it is difficult to find books if you don't know how to use it. Here is a list of things you should know in order to find a nonfiction book in your library:

- Books are cataloged alphabetically in three ways: by *author* (last name), by *title,* and by *subject.*

- Each book is given a "call number" which is based on the Dewey decimal classification system. The first three numbers tell what a particular book is about:
  000–099 : Generalities
  100–199 : Philosophy
  200–299 : Religion
  300–399 : Social sciences
  400–499 : Languages
  500–599 : Pure sciences
  600–699 : Technology or applied sciences
  700–799 : The arts
  800–899 : Literature and rhetoric
  900–999 : General geography, history, etc.

- The library is divided into sections, based upon the Dewey decimal numbers. For example, if the first three numbers of a book are 250, that book will be in the 200–299 (religion) section of the library. *Get to know the arrangement of your library!*

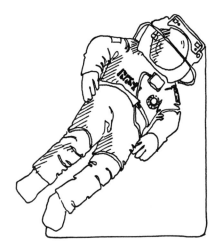

- Once you have found the proper section of the library, use the rest of the call number to locate the book on the shelves.

The cards for books that Jerome found at the library

```
629.475

V891r     Von Braun, Wernher, 1912–
              The rocket's red glare/Wernher von
          Braun and Frederick I. Ordway III., 1st ed.,
          Garden City, N.Y. : Anchor Press, 1976.


              212 p. illus.
              Bibliography: p. 191–204
              Includes index
```

READING MATERIAL, CONT'D

629.1331   Handbook of model rocketry:

St56h

1983   Stine, George Harry, 1928–
            Handbook of model rocketry; NAR official
        handbook by G. Harry Stine. 5th ed. completely
        rev. N.Y., Arco Pub., Inc. 1983.

            367 p. illus., plans
            Bibliography: p. 333.
            Includes index

ROCKETS (AERONAUTICS)

629.434
C174s   Caprara, Giovanni
            The complete encyclopedia of space
        satellites. N.Y., Portland House, 1986.

            219 p. illus.
            Bibliography: p. 219
            Includes index

ROCKETS (AERONAUTICS)

629.475

G226m   Gatland, Kenneth 1924–
            Missiles and rockets. N.Y., Macmillan
        Pub. Co., Inc., 1975.

            256 p. illus.
            Includes index

ROCKETS (AERONAUTICS)

629.44   Smith, Melvyn
Sm62s   An illustrated history of space shuttle.
        Newbury Park, CA, Haynes Pub., Inc., 1985.

            246 p. illus.
            Includes index

Name _____ Date _____

CLASSROOM ASSIGNMENT

Answer the following questions by referring to the information in
the reading material, and by using your knowledge of finding books
in the library. Keep in mind that the ability to locate information is
an essential research skill.

1. In what section of the library will all of Jerome's books be
   found?

   _____

2. Which of Jerome's books was most recently published?

   _____

3. Which of Jerome's books is the least current?

   _____

4. Which book has more than one author? Who are the authors?

   _____

   _____

5. List each of the five books and tell if Jerome found it on an author, subject, or title
   card.

Title	*Type of Card*
_____	_____
_____	_____
_____	_____
_____	_____
_____	_____

6. Which book provides plans for building a rocket?

   _____

7. What does "illus." on a catalog card mean?

   _____

8. What is a bibliography?

   _____

   _____

CLASSROOM ASSIGNMENT, CONT'D

9. What does the letter (or letters) at the beginning of the second part of each call number stand for?

_____

10. Organize the following call numbers, as they would be on a library shelf, by numbering them 1–10 in the spaces provided: "1" is the first book you would find on the shelf, and "10" is the last book.

_____ 629.475 V89lr	_____ 629.1131 St56h	_____ 629.201 D118f	_____ 629.1131 D68n
_____ 629.1326 B618s	_____ 629.617 R87b	_____ 629.475 G226m	
_____ 629.617 R131h	_____ 629.434 C174s	_____ 629.44 Sm62s	

Name _____ Date _____

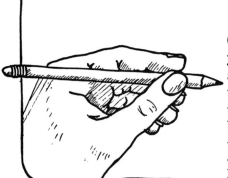

ON YOUR OWN

Choose a topic from the list below. Conduct a catalog search at your local public library for books that contain information about the topic you have chosen. In the spaces provided, record the call number, the author(s), and the title for each of ten books that you find in the catalog. You need not check these books out, but it would be a good idea to locate them to help you learn about the arrangement of the various sections of your library and to prove that you know how to track down specific call numbers. If the catalog does not contain ten books about your topic, record what is available and then choose a second topic to complete the assignment. Note: some libraries use the Library of Congress method rather than the Dewey Decimal system to catalog books. Ask the librarian to help you if you get confused.

TOPICS

World War I	Mammals	China
World War II	Insects	Presidents, U.S.
Automobiles	Birds	Rocks and minerals
Dance	Fish	Dinosaurs
Music	Islam	Judaism
Airplanes	Biology	Middle East
Christianity	England	Chemistry
Oceans	Guns	Education
Astronomy	Ships and boats	French (language)
Folk stories	Stamps	Japanese (language)
The Civil War	Coins	Sculpture
Greek philosophers	Psychology	Trains and railroads
Renaissance art	Trees	Maps and mapping
Electricity	Vietnam	Roman Empire
Basketball	Football	Agriculture
Abraham Lincoln	George Washington	Pollution
Economics	Reptiles	Flowers
Architecture	Archaeology	Native Americans
Explorers	Inventors	Games
Pioneers	Mexico	Computers

Topic choice No. 1 _____

Topic choice No. 2 _____
(if necessary)

ON YOUR OWN, CONT'D

Call No.	Author(s)	Title
1. _____	_____	_____
_____	_____	_____
2. _____	_____	_____
_____	_____	_____
3. _____	_____	_____
_____	_____	_____
4. _____	_____	_____
_____	_____	_____
5. _____	_____	_____
_____	_____	_____
6. _____	_____	_____
_____	_____	_____
7. _____	_____	_____
_____	_____	_____
8. _____	_____	_____
_____	_____	_____
9. _____	_____	_____
_____	_____	_____
10. _____	_____	_____
_____	_____	_____

ACTIVITY 4.
Making Use of Your Time

TEACHER PREVIEW

LESSON DESCRIPTIONS

Introductory Narrative ("Time's a-Wastin'"): Anne tells of her inclination to waste time and her realization that she should make better use of it. She accepts her mother's challenge to record her daily activities.

Reading Material: Anne's "Daily Agenda" chart and an excerpt from her journal. The chart is a schedule of her daily activities and the time spent on each.

Classroom Assignment: Through class discussion, students make a "Daily Agenda" for a typical student, then work on their own agendas using a provided chart. Agendas may be discussed in class.

On Your Own: Students organize a promotional campaign to encourage people to spend their time in productive, creative, fulfilling ways. Each student (1) writes a classified ad for the "Wanted: People Willing to Share" section of the newspaper, and (2) produces a pamphlet or brochure describing a specific activity in which other students may be interested.

SUGGESTIONS FOR SETTING THE STAGE

- Initiate a discussion about time management. Talk about the value of making good use of your time: the things that can be accomplished, pursued, and learned. As a class, develop a list of specific activities, hobbies, areas of knowledge, experiences, sports, arts, clubs, organizations, career goals, and so forth that would provide students with interesting and useful things to do with their time. Have students record the list that is created for use with *Classroom Assignment* and *On Your Own*.

- Tell the class a story:

  A student from the class (choose somebody and use his or her name) found an old lamp at a flea market, bought it, and took it home. Upon trying to buff it clean, a genie appeared and offered the student one wish, which would be granted if it could be shown that it was not selfish. The student thought and thought, then said "I wish there were twenty-five hours in a day. How can it be selfish if everyone in the whole world benefits?" The genie couldn't argue with that, and it was so.

Instruct the class to spend five or ten minutes writing about what they will do with their extra hour each day. Then have a discussion or let students read their answers orally.

Name _____   Date _____

INTRODUCTORY NARRATIVE

Read the following narrative to find out how Anne came to the realization that she was wasting a lot of her precious time.

Time's a-Wastin'
by Anne

Wasting time used to be my main hobby. I mean, I spent hours and hours doing things that were so meaningless they left no memory at all. It's difficult to recall what I did with a lot of my vacation time, evenings, weekends, and even school time. "Hanging out," "messing around," and "nothing," were my usual responses when asked what I was doing. Mom and Dad made quite a fuss over my refusal to make good use of my time. "Time is precious," my mom would say. "Time is our most valuable commodity," my dad would say. "Yeah, yeah, yeah," I would say (under my breath).

One day as I was lying around the living room doing nothing, my mom sat down next to me with that "let's talk" look in her eye. It was the same old stuff, but with a new twist. She challenged me to carefully and honestly keep track of everything I did for a week and record how much time was devoted to each activity. She asked me to make a chart showing my typical daily schedule and the number of minutes I spent on each item. She said I could learn a lot about myself with this project.

I agreed to chart my "daily agenda" to keep Mom off my back, but soon I became really interested in taking a closer look at how I was living my life. I was amazed at the results, especially when they were projected to show how much time I would spend (or waste!) on certain things by the time I'm twenty-one. As a result of this "assignment" I have changed my opinion about the importance of trying to make better use of my time. Maybe it's because I'm getting older, but now I think more about being productive and less about how to get out of work. I am more concerned with improving myself and setting goals than I am with just having a good time and doing whatever I feel like doing (which I found out was quite often *nothing*!). I'm determined to improve the quality of my life by making better use of my time.

Mom says time is precious, and I agree. A person grows up pretty quickly in this world, and it shouldn't be done sitting down. My advice to my friends and people my age is: let's take advantage of what we've got. Time's a-wastin'!

Name _____ Date _____

READING MATERIAL

Students have access to the world's most valuable commodity: time. Although it may sound insincere or even corny to urge students to make productive use of their time, the advice is seriously given. A person can't be *forced* to see the logic in learning to do productive or creative things with his or her time, but some of the advantages should be obvious. Studying, performing, creating, developing, designing, investigating, exploring, organizing, building, collecting, presenting, learning: *time* allows these things to occur, and it really does feel good to be engaged in such undertakings.

Anyone who decides to alter how he or she makes use of time can do so by pursuing interesting, challenging, informative, creative, or productive activities during the time that is available. This leads to personal pride and satisfaction, a sense of task-commitment, and an increased level of self-confidence, all of which are important characteristics of a successful person in the modern world.

The chart below shows how Anne spent time during a typical day. It also shows how much time she would have devoted to each activity in a year and by the time she was 21, if she continued to live in the same way. Following the chart is an excerpt from Anne's journal, giving some comments about her "Time's a-Wastin'" project.

Daily Agenda	Minutes/Day	Minutes/Year	Between Now and age 21
School time: productive (classes and school activities, 185 days/year)	270	49,950	349,650
School time: nonproductive (wasted study time, goofing off, etc. 185 days/year)	30	5,550	38,850
Eating (3 meals/day, 365 days/year)	60	21,900	153,300
Walking/riding bus to and from school (185 days/year)	40	7,400	51,800
Homework (185 days/year)	45	8,325	58,275
Being distracted from homework (185 days/year)	15	2,775	19,425

READING MATERIAL, CONT'D

Daily Agenda	Minutes/Day	Minutes/Year	Between Now and age 21
Complaining about having to get up (185 days/year)	15	2,775	19,425
Talking on the telephone (365 days/year)	30	10,950	76,650
Going with friends to the mall (about 3 hrs/week, 52 weeks/year)	25	9,125	63,875
Watching T.V. (365 days/year)	180	65,700	459,900
Avoiding or putting off doing chores (365 days/year)	20	7,300	51,100
Doing chores (365 days/year)	30	10,950	76,650
Listening to music while doing nothing else (365 days/year)	60	21,900	153,300
Hanging around waiting for something to happen (365 days/year)	45	16,425	114,975
Lying on my bed, daydreaming (usually without music: 365 days/year)	20	7,300	51,100
Arguing and fighting with my brother and sister (365 days/year)	15	5,475	38,325
Worrying about things that don't matter (365 days/year)	30	10,950	76,650
Sleeping (365 days/year)	480	175,200	1,226,400
Weekend and vacation "free time" (time I can spend any way I want, 180 days/year) 104 weekend days 76 vacation days	360	64,800	453,600

READING MATERIAL, CONT'D

Journal entry, April 16, 1989

I am amazed at how much time I have and how little of it I use wisely. When mom challenged me to do this project, I thought it was a joke, but it wasn't. The chart I made shows my life, not some boring research assignment. When I look at it I see myself stumbling through another day without really getting anywhere. This is going to end! Who would have thought that every year I watch television for 65,700 minutes. At that rate I will watch 7,665 *hours* of television between now and my twenty-first birthday. That's equal to 319 twenty-four–hour days! In a single year I complain about getting out of bed for 2,775 minutes, fight with my brother and sister for 5,475 minutes, and try to get out of doing chores for 7,300 minutes. Total: 15,550 minutes, or 259 hours. Can you imagine complaining for 46 hours about having to get up?

A real pattern of wasted time became clear to me as I worked on this project. I spent around 45 minutes every day just waiting for something to happen, or for someone to stop by or call. Usually nothing happened, so I would listen to music or lie on my bed daydreaming. Total time per day: at *least* 90 minutes. If I had kept this up, my chart shows that by the time I turned 21 I would have "hung around" for 114,975 minutes, waiting for someone else to make something happen in my life

The chart shows a lot of things, but my last comment about it deals with weekend and vacation time: 64,800 minutes per year are available to me, with really only myself to count on to make them worthwhile. This fact never occurred to me before, but now that it has, I intend to do something about it. Some of my ideas include reading good books, starting a hobby, studying subjects that interest me, joining a club, taking up a musical instrument (probably guitar), working to get better grades, going out for a sports team, finding out about social events, becoming involved in community activities, and preparing in whatever ways I can for my career goals. I also intend to have fun with my friends, continue listening to music, and daydream once in a while. I'm not cutting out all the good times, I'm just expanding and adding to them.

Name _____ Date _____

CLASSROOM ASSIGNMENT

- In a class discussion, make a daily agenda for a fictional classmate. What kinds of things do most people your age spend their time doing? Describe a typical day in terms of minutes spent on each activity.

- Record your own daily agenda on the chart provided. Think carefully about what your daily schedule looks like, and be as detailed as possible. Your agenda will include activities that you do regularly, but not necessarily every day. To calculate minutes per year, multiply minutes per day by the number of days out of the year you do a particular thing.

  - Every day, multiply by 365.
  - Every *school* day, multiply by 185.
  - Every *weekend* day, multiply by 104.
  - Every *vacation* day, multiply by 76.
  - One day a week, multiply by 52.
  - Once a week during the school year, multiply by 37.
  - Once a month, multiply by 12.

- At the bottom of your Daily Agenda, record two activities, projects, hobbies, or areas of interest that you would like to build into your life. How can this be done? Look at your Daily Agenda to see if there is time available. If not, can anything be dropped from your present schedule to make room for new undertakings?

- Be prepared to discuss your Daily Agenda in class, especially parts of the schedule that you feel are not productive or that could be eliminated. What would you replace these items with? How would you rather be spending your time?

Name _____ **Date** _____

Grade _____

Age _____

DAILY AGENDA

Activities	Days/Year	Min./Day	Min./Year	Between Now and Age 21(yrs)
_____				
_____				
_____				
_____				
_____				
_____				
_____				
_____				
_____				
_____				
_____				
_____				
_____				
_____				

Possible additions to the agenda:

1. _____

_____

2. _____

_____

© 1990 by The Center for Applied Research in Education

Name _____ Date _____

ON YOUR OWN

Your class is organizing a promotional campaign to encourage people to spend their time in productive, creative, fulfilling ways. Your assignment has two parts:

1. To convince people that they have skills, knowledge, interests, gifts, and talents worth sharing with others, your class will produce a section of classified ads for an imaginary newspaper. The classified section is "Wanted: People Willing to Share." You will write *one* advertisement.

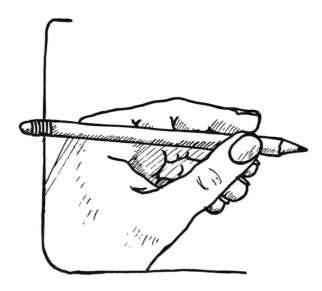

a. Choose something that either you personally, or a person for whom you are writing, would like to learn from someone else. For example:

- Knowledge about a specific topic (astronomy or cars)
- Experience with certain situations (losing a good friend or having divorced parents)
- A particular hobby (photography or stamp collecting)
- A special skill or talent (being good at mathematics or playing the piano)
- Connections to a group or organization (Girl Scouts or the Camera Club)

b. Write a classified ad. Begin with "Wanted: A person . . ." and explain precisely what you are looking for.

- Why do you need this particular type of person?
- What will he or she do for you?
- Explain where/when/how you want to meet or communicate.
- Describe the time commitment that will be required of the person who answers your ad. A math tutor might be needed for an hour a week for a semester; a request for a close and confidential friend would require a full-time commitment.

c. Your classified ad should be one paragraph long and written as concisely as possible. It will be turned in, and it may be put on display in the room.

ON YOUR OWN, CONT'D

2. Produce a pamphlet or brochure that promotes one activity that would be a productive, creative, or satisfying use of time for someone your age.

   a. Choose an activity that you either know about from personal experience and would recommend to others, or that you would like to know more about because it sounds interesting.

   b. Your pamphlet or brochure should be informative. Conduct some research to be sure you have accurate information. Talk to people and go to the library to collect material for your final product.

   c. Explain to the reader (the person who picks up your pamphlet) why he or she might be interested in the activity you are describing. Why do people enjoy participating in it?

   d. Describe the steps a person must follow to become good at or deeply interested in the activity.

   e. Some suggestions to get you thinking:

   • Coin collecting

   • Model trains

   • Reading about history

   • Clubs or scouts

   • Drawing and painting

   • Golf

   • Photography

   • Politics

   • Computers

   • Poetry

ACTIVITY 5.
Creating a Script

TEACHER PREVIEW

LESSON DESCRIPTIONS

Introductory Narrative ("The Show Must Go On"): Kim explains why she and her friends decided to produce a "Summer Playhouse" in her backyard to help raise money for their local Students Against Drunk Drivers (SADD) organization.

Reading Material: Kim's script, "The Trial." This play can be produced in a classroom. It also can lead to a class discussion about what Kim was trying to say with her play.

Classroom Assignment: Students develop introductions to plays that they would like to write: title, characters, setting, stage arrangement, general story description, and initial dialogue. Discussion in class centers on story descriptions.

On Your Own: Students write their own one-act plays. Kim's play (provided as Reading Material) can serve as a model for this lesson. Material for the play may be taken from the Classroom Assignment or it may be developed from new ideas.

SUGGESTIONS FOR SETTING THE STAGE

- Bring the script for a play to class for students to sight-read. Assign parts and let the "characters" read their parts from the front of the room. Discuss how the readers knew when to be angry, sad, surprised, gloomy, and so forth. How does a playwright tell a director and actors about the characters' moods, behaviors, and actions? How about settings and stage arrangements? Discuss the mechanics of writing a play.

- Bring a play to class for students to sight-read. Be careful in your selection; try to choose a play that lends itself to a discussion of what the author was trying to say. This should lead to a discussion of motivation: Why do people write plays? What makes them do it? What are they trying to accomplish? Make a list of "reasons for writing," and have students identify one or more that might lead them to write a play.

- Take the class to a dramatic reading, school musical, class play, community play, or professional production. Then discuss what is required to produce such a show in terms of script, props, costumes, scenery, makeup, lighting, sound effects, and music. Impress upon the students that creativity is called for in scriptwriting, but also in each of the other areas mentioned above. Use this introduction to theater to help motivate them to write plays of their own.

Name _____ Date _____

INTRODUCTORY NARRATIVE

Read the following narrative to find out what motivated Kim and her friends to write their own plays for presentation in a backyard "Summer Playhouse."

The Show Must Go On
by Kim

Last February was a dreary, depressing, lonely month. I almost lost my best friend Carol in a car accident, and I sat around day after day worrying about her. Would she live? Would she ever walk again? Would she recover and be the same old Carol? Gradually she got better, and one day in early March she was allowed to go home from the hospital. She may have to walk with a cane for the rest of her life, and she has scars on her forehead, right cheek, and chin, but her spirit is strong and she is very happy to be alive. All of her friends are happy, too.

What does Carol's accident have to do with our Summer Playhouse? Everything. You see, Carol's accident was caused by a drunk driver. He ran a stoplight and plowed into the passenger side of her dad's car. Carol was almost killed, but the drunk driver didn't get a scratch, and the next day he claimed to have no memory of the accident. That's when I joined Students Against Drunk Drivers (SADD), along with some of my friends. We were angry about the senseless destruction caused by alcohol related accidents, especially our near loss of Carol, and we *had* to do something. Anyway, this summer our local SADD organization asked all its members to help raise money for a fall public relations campaign titled "Don't Let Them Drive." My friends and I decided to create a Summer Playhouse by producing our own plays on a backyard stage. The proceeds all went to SADD.

Organizing a backyard theater is not easy. We had to set up a stage, make props, design scenery, find costumes, arrange seating for the audience, and of course, write plays. There are published plays available, but we all felt that we wanted to try writing our own. My brother showed us how scripts are written, and he let us look at some books of plays that came from his drama class. He was very helpful in teaching us how to organize our plays on paper. In his words, he taught us a "simple format."

The stage was the area directly behind the garage. The garage wall gave us a place to hang or attach scenery. Two trees about fifteen feet from the wall became the posts for our curtain: we stretched a rope between them and hung blankets from it. The audience sat on the other side of the curtain in donated lawn chairs. We used puppets in some of our plays, so we put a puppet stage directly in front of the curtain, just to the right of the stage. It was a refrigerator box (which we got from a local appliance store) with the upper half of one panel cut out, and a bath towel hung across the opening to serve as a curtain. The puppet operators were hidden in the lower half of the box.

Finding props made us use our imaginations. For example, driving a car was shown by sitting on a chair, holding a garbage pail lid at arm's length with both hands, and turning it back and forth slightly. If we wanted a prop that was impossible to produce, we would draw it on posterboard and hold it up for the audience to see. That's what we did when we needed a whale for one scene. Under a picture of a whale were the words "Action takes place on the back of a whale." Background scenery was usually done with posters or pieces of butcher paper that had drawings or words that helped the audience visualize the scene. Costumes were whatever we could scrounge up, like the rope mop we used as witches' hair.

As you may be able to tell, I enjoyed working on our Summer Playhouse, and I'm sorry it's over. But what I'm really happy about is that Carol is still my best friend and we had a blast just being together. It would have been an unbearable tragedy if that drunk man had been able to put an end to our friendship. That's why I'm going to continue doing what I can to put an end to drunk driving. Nobody should have to experience such a tragedy.

Name ————————————————— Date —————————————

READING MATERIAL

If you have something to say, writing a play is a good method of self-expression. You can invent characters and have them say and do whatever you please. They can live anywhere in the world, in any time period. Sitting down at a blank piece of paper, you have the power to create people, places, events, and entire new worlds. Even if you would not list "playwright" in your top 100 occupational choices and have never considered trying your hand at writing a script for a play, you should give it at least one good effort. Who knows—there might be a talent lurking deep down inside, just waiting for an opportunity to make itself known.

Kim and her friends were first-time playwrights. Their desire to write came from anger at what happened to Carol, mixed with desire to do something meaningful in the fight against drunk driving. Motivation is a key element of good writing. Without it, most writing lacks vitality and creative flair. As you read Kim's play, keep in mind what her motivation was and see if you can think of situations that might provide you with incentive to write.

THE TRIAL
by Kim L. Shelby

Characters

PUPPET 1
PUPPET 2
JUDGE, *supreme judge of the "People of the Vale"*
SOLICITOR, *chief representative of the "People of the Vale"*
RAPAZING, *the defendant*
GRENISHOD, *Rapazing's friend*
WITNESS 1
WITNESS 2
SEVERAL SPECTATORS

Scene 1

Setting: A puppet stage.
At Rise: Two puppets on stage, talking to each other. PUPPET 1 *is telling* PUPPET 2 *a story, being very emphatic and animated.*
PUPPET 1: . . . And that's the end of my story. It was the most amazing thing ever seen in the Land of Sand. I tell you, no one's seen the like.
PUPPET 2: I have a story that might win the honor of "most amazing" once it's told. It's about the first age and the people who lived here long ago.
PUPPET 1: First age? What's that?
PUPPET 2: There was a time when this valley was more than dunes and sand. Beautiful as they are, this country was once even more spectacular. Imagine streams and waterfalls, trees and lush meadows, and a river winding through the floor of the valley. Animals of all types lived here, and the people were peaceful and law abiding.
PUPPET 1: People?
PUPPET 2: Yes. People of the Vale. They lived here during the first age. They were a magical people. I mean, they had control over natural things in a way that we can't imagine today.

READING MATERIAL, CONT'D

If they needed rain, they made it rain. It's said they could turn rocks into gold and sand into fertile soil. They were very mystical.

PUPPET 1: What happened to them?

PUPPET 2: That's my story. Let me tell you about The Trial.

Curtain

* * *

Scene 2

Setting: The Supreme Courtroom of the People of Vale.

At Rise: WITNESS 1 *is on the stand, being questioned by the* SOLICITOR. *The* JUDGE *is on a thronelike seat, the defendant is sitting alone, and* GRENISHOD, WITNESS 2, *and the* SPECTATORS *are sitting together.*

SOLICITOR (*To the judge*): One final question and I will be through with this witness Your Honor. (*Turns to the witness*) You've told us you saw the defendant in the Darkling Forest. What was he doing?

WITNESS 1 (*Pauses and glances secretively from side to side*): He was . . . (*Another pause*) He was milking the blossoms of enchantment plants to get nectar; he was taking it from *my* land. (*Everyone gasps, then begins to whisper.*) He was collecting the wine of power!

JUDGE (*Raps a gavel on the arm of the throne and speaks to the witness*): Do you realize what you are saying? For eons it has been forbidden to possess enchantment nectar. It is a danger to our entire civilization. Are you certain of this charge you are making?

WITNESS 1: Your Honor, I've sworn to tell the truth and I'm tellin' it. I saw what I saw and I'm tellin' what I saw. I can't do any more than that.

JUDGE: Very well. Solicitor, continue with your case.

SOLICITOR: I call my next witness to the stand. (WITNESS 2 *trades places with* WITNESS 1) You are a mysticologist, is that right?

WITNESS 2: That is correct. I am in charge of monitoring the use of magic in the Land of Vale.

SOLICITOR: Can you explain in plain language why the possession of enchantment nectar is forbidden?

WITNESS 2: The wine of power alters how people think. It actually changes their minds, but not in ways that are obvious. It casts a spell on the brain. Once a person begins drinking enchantment nectar, it is impossible to stop. This person will also refuse to admit to using it.

SOLICITOR: Why is it a danger to our entire civilization?

WITNESS 2: We live in a magical valley. Everyone is so familiar with magic that it doesn't even occur to them that things around here are *unusual*. We can make it rain over just one field if it needs water. We can ask a tree to produce fruit and it will, instantly. We can make things float through the air from one place to another. We can . . .

SOLICITOR: (*Impatiently*) Yes, yes, yes . . . We all know of these ordinary occurrences. What does this have to do with enchantment nectar and dangers to the People of the Vale?

WITNESS 2: There is other magic at work here. This valley is not what it appears to be. Without magic, we would be surrounded by sand, nothing but dunes and dryness. Life as we know it would be impossible. Our land is kept lush and green, beautiful beyond words, by the combined magic of all the people.

SOLICITOR: Are you saying that the Vale is what it is because we *think* it is?

READING MATERIAL, CONT'D

WITNESS 2: That's one way of putting it. Each person, every one of us, has a natural, subconcious, built-in, instinctive desire to keep the valley exactly as it is. Every single one of us focuses a portion of our magic on making the valley remain as it was last year and a hundred years ago. We don't even know we're doing it.

JUDGE: (*Thoughtfully*) I see. It's genetic. We can't help it. Each of us contributes to making this valley what it is without even thinking about it. You are saying that, without our magic, the valley would change, is that right?

WITNESS 2: Correct. And that's where enchantment nectar comes in. A person who drinks it gradually loses his instinctive desire to keep the valley the same. In fact, he might even decide that he would like to *change* it! (*Everyone in the courtroom murmurs and glances nervously around the room.*)

JUDGE: That's bad. That's bad. That's not good. That's bad . . . (*Noticing that she's babbling*) Solicitor, call your next witness.

SOLICITOR: I call Grenishod, the defendant's friend. (GRENISHOD *trades places with* WITNESS 2) You *are* the defendant's friend, are you not?

GRENISHOD: Yes. Rapazing and I have been very good friends almost since we were born.

SOLICITOR: Did you know that Rapazing was milking enchantment plants and drinking the nectar?

GRENISHOD (*Pauses and looks at* RAPAZING *then lowers his eyes*) Yes. For quite some time.

SOLICITOR: Did you notice any changes in his behavior over that time?

GRENISHOD: Not really. He kept wanting more and more enchantment nectar. I went with him a few times to collect it.

SOLICITOR: Come, now, Grenishod. There were never moments of odd behavior?

GRENISHOD: Not until recently. Now he denies his use of nectar, even while he drinks it. He claims it is ping ping juice. And, just last week, we went for a walk and he said it would be nice if the woods weren't so overgrown. He tried to use magic to remove some trees, and for a few moments all the trees on one hillside disappeared and were replaced by sand. Then he sat down and held his head, and the trees reappeared. He took a drink of nectar and seemed to be all right, but he wanted to go right home. I haven't seen him since, until today.

SOLICITOR: Thank you Grenishod. That will be all. I now call the defendant, Rapazing. (GRENISHOD *sits down and* RAPAZING *takes the stand.*) Rapazing, do you deny any of the things that have been said here today?

RAPAZING: I drink ping ping juice, not nectar.

SOLICITOR: Come, come, Rapazing; admit it. Ping ping juice and enchantment nectar are the same thing!

RAPAZING: I see nothing wrong with ping ping juice. You people think things always must remain the same, but I don't. Ping ping juice makes you feel good. It makes the world a better place to live in. It helps you realize how things could be changed and improved. I'm glad I tried it years ago; I could really use some right now.

SOLICITOR: Don't you care that it's a danger to our society?

RAPAZING: That's just an unproven theory. And don't sound so high and mighty. There are other people, right in this room, who have tried ping ping juice. (*Everyone glances around with a look of surprise.*)

SOLICITOR: We've heard enough! For my final witness I wish to recall our mysticologist. (WITNESS 2 *comes to the stand,* RAPAZING *returns to the defendant's chair.*) You've heard all the evidence; now I ask for advice. What should be done to protect the Land and People of Vale?

READING MATERIAL, CONT'D

WITNESS 2: One, or two, or three people drinking enchantment nectar will not endanger our society, but if it becomes widespread, it's a different story. Then, each person will decide things should be different and there will be no agreement. If such an unlikely thing should happen, our valley will become sand. My advice is to place RAPAZING under arrest, confine him to his house, and prevent him from drinking the nectar. Then the rest of us can forget about this nasty little incident.

JUDGE: In your opinion, are there others in the valley who are drinking enchantment nectar?

WITNESS 2: I do not think so. I believe everything is just fine in our world; couldn't be better!

JUDGE: Let it be as you have said. Confine Rapazing to his own house. Thank goodness the People of the Vale do not have a problem with enchantment nectar. Court is adjourned. (*Everyone in the room breathes a sigh of relief, gets up, moves to different parts of the stage, and looks around to make sure nobody is watching. Then, all at the same time, each person reaches in his or her pocket, removes a flask, and takes a long, hard drink while making noises of satisfaction, rubbing stomachs, and giving signs of finally quenching a great thirst.*)

Curtain

* * *

Scene 3

Setting: A puppet stage.
At Rise: PUPPET 2 *is finishing the story about The Trial, as* PUPPET 1 *listens.*

PUPPET 2 (*In a sad voice*): So, everyone went happily off, convinced that the problem was taken care of, when in fact it was simply well disguised. Refusing to admit that there was trouble down the road, the People of the Vale, and the Vale itself, gradually faded away. I've heard that the last few, living in a sandy wasteland and running out of enchantment plants, actually wished themselves out of existence, and so they disappeared for ever. It's a sad ending.

PUPPET 1: Yes, very sad . . . but, (*voice brightens*) their loss was our gain. Look at all of this beautiful sand. It's enough to satisfy the desires of anyone. I think I prefer to be happy with what I've got and have no possibility of making changes than to have the power to change things and blow it. That enchantment nectar took away their ability to think straight; it ruined them. None of that for me, thank you.

PUPPET 2: I agree. Yes, indeed, I certainly do agree.

The End

Name ——————————————————— **Date** ———————————————————

CLASSROOM ASSIGNMENT

This worksheet will help as you prepare to write a script of your own. Follow the directions and consider each part carefully before recording your responses. Remember that time and effort are necessary to produce a good script. It is a complex undertaking that requires a certain amount of motivation and commitment; be prepared to spend time *thinking* about this assignment, to guarantee a quality product.

I. Develop an introduction to a play. If you were going to write a play, what would its title be? What characters would you use? Where would the play take place? What would the stage look like when the curtain rises at the beginning of the play?

TITLE: ——————————————————————————————

AUTHOR: —————————————————————————————

CHARACTERS (at least 3): ——————————————————

——————————————————————————————————

——————————————————————————————————

——————————————————————————————————

——————————————————————————————————

——————————————————————————————————

——————————————————————————————————

——————————————————————————————————

SETTING: —————————————————————————————

——————————————————————————————————

——————————————————————————————————

——————————————————————————————————

——————————————————————————————————

——————————————————————————————————

——————————————————————————————————

CLASSROOM ASSIGNMENT, CONT'D

AT RISE: _____

_____

_____

_____

_____

_____

_____

II. On a separate piece of paper, describe the story you would tell with your play. Tell only the main theme, moral, plot, or situation that your play would present. In other words, explain briefly what it is about. Remember, this is an *imaginary* play. You haven't written it, but you are describing it as if you have.

III. On a separate piece of paper, record the first five or six lines of dialogue from the play you are developing. You have described what the stage will look like when the curtain rises. Now record what the audience will hear:

CHARACTER 1:

CHARACTER 2:

CHARACTER 3:

CHARACTER 2:

And so forth . . .

    It is important to include directions for action or expression at the appropriate places by including them in parentheses. See Kim's play for examples.

IV. Be prepared to describe your story (part II) to the class in a general discussion about ideas for plays. This is laying the groundwork for actually writing a play of your own. Sharing ideas with others is a good way of preparing yourself to begin such an undertaking.

Name _____ **Date** _____

ON YOUR OWN

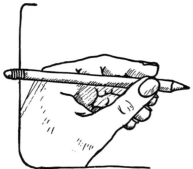

Write a script for a one-act play. Record the introductory material on this assignment sheet, and then continue on lined paper to complete the play. You may use the material from the Classroom Assignment, or you may decide to start over with a new idea. Your play should be a *minimum* of three pages long (this page plus three pages of dialogue).

TITLE: _____

by: _____

Characters

_____

_____

_____

_____

_____

_____

SCENE 1

SETTING: _____

_____

_____

AT RISE: _____

_____

_____

_____

_____

_____

ACTIVITY 6.
Writing a Business Letter

TEACHER PREVIEW

LESSON DESCRIPTIONS

Introductory Narrative ("Sincerely Yours"): Felicia tells why she had to learn how to write a business letter in order to apply for a grant to help her study literature.

Reading Material: Basic information about business letters, followed by copies of letters by Mr. Coole and Felicia. These letters are modified block, mixed punctuation, and can be used as models for students to follow as they write their own letters.

Classroom Assignment: Students write business letters based upon four scenarios described on the lesson sheet. Each student chooses one scenario from which to work.

On Your Own: Students create hypothetical situations that lead people to write business letters. They describe the person to whom the letter is sent and the person who is writing the letter. Then they write business letters that fit the scenarios they have developed.

SUGGESTIONS FOR SETTING THE STAGE

- Bring samples of letterhead stationery to class for students to look at and discuss. Are some more effective than others at "grabbing your attention?" What is the value of a letterhead? Why is it important for a business letter to look sharp and professional? What is the purpose of a business letter? Let the variety of letterheads lead to a discussion of business letters. To get letterhead stationery, ask companies and professionals to donate copies, or inquire at print shops for samples of their work.

- In a class discussion, invent a fictional company: name, products, president, location, subsidiaries, etc. Then have students design letterhead stationery for the company.

- Compose a business letter that is intentionally vague, contradictory, or incomplete. Give students five minutes to write down what they think the letter says. Then compare interpretations and discuss the need for clarity and uniformity in business letters. For example:

Dear Mr. Brown:

I am very interested in meeting your terms. It is my area of expertise. Do you want me to work or will you let me know when I should start and what I should do? I'm anxious to improve my qualifications if you choose me. I will give you a call.

Meanwhile, please remember my experience. Your product needs my knowledge. I will accept a salary comparable to the ones being earned by qualified persons in equivalent occupations in other fields of endeavor (with experience levels similar to mine) unless, of course, this makes my employment less likely. Please take my serious comments into consideration.

I am anxiously awaiting a return call from you, and hope to hear from you soon. My employer needs your business, so stay in touch. Without people like us, people like you can get hurt, if you know what I mean. Anyway, if I don't receive a communication from you in two weeks, I will take my business elsewhere, because I'm convinced that I need you at least as much as you need me.

I've enjoyed doing business with you.

Sincerely,

Mr. Smith

Name _____ Date _____

INTRODUCTORY NARRATIVE

Read the following narrative for an explanation of Felicia's sudden interest in writing a business letter.

Sincerely Yours
by Felicia

Who would have thought that my fascination with books would lead me to learn about business letters? Until a few months ago I had no interest at all in such things, but that changed when I applied for a grant of $100 to pursue my interest in literature. Suddenly the ability to write a business letter became all-important, because that's what I had to do to even be considered for the grant. Let me explain.

One day my English teacher told us that a local corporation was offering grants to students who had special interests in science, mathematics, history, or literature. If we wanted more information we could take a sheet from her desk as we left class. I took one. It said to fill out a form with your name, address, phone number, grade, and age, and send it to the president of UltraCom, Inc. I sent the form, and about two weeks later I received a formal, typewritten business letter from Mr. Jonathan S. Coole, President, UltraCom, Inc. He explained that his company was offering grants to students as a way of promoting good communication skills. He said he and other business people were thinking of creative ways to get young people to communicate with others. His idea was to offer grant money to local students. To obtain the money, interested students would be required to write business letters explaining why they want it and how it would be used. This way, he was emphasizing communication *and* encouraging students to learn more about science, mathematics, history, and literature.

I decided to try for a grant. Mr. Coole was offering a total of fifty-six $100 grants (two in each subject area for each grade, 6–12). This meant my proposal was in competition with everyone in my grade who was applying for a literature grant. Since the award was based solely on the quality of the business letter proposal, my first task was to find out how to organize and compose a business letter. I did that by checking a book out of the library called *Reference Manual for Office Workers* by Louis C. Nanassy, William Selden, and Jo Ann Lee. It had all the information I needed about business letters.

Next, I had to decide what to say. Writing a brief, informative, persuasive letter is not easy. I spent a lot of time writing letters that ended up as crumpled balls in my wastebasket. Finally my mom came to the rescue. She pointed out that I was thinking like a student instead of like a business person. I was approaching the project as an assignment rather than as a personal challenge. Mom told me to look upon it as a professional undertaking, just as if I were seeking employment or trying to land a contract or attempting to sell a manuscript. Her suggestion worked. By thinking about it differently, I was able to compose a pretty good letter. I guess it was good, anyway. I was awarded the grant money and now I'm busy studying the things I love: good books.

Name _____ **Date** _____

READING MATERIAL

There are many situations in the modern world that require communicating with people you hardly know or don't know at all. This communication is often done through the mail, by writing letters. A business letter can be used to request information, offer services, sell products, ask advice, make suggestions, state opinions, coordinate activities, promote ideas, respond to previous correspondence, or introduce yourself to others. A person with the ability to compose a well written business letter is in a strong position to get what he or she wants. That is the kind of skill worth acquiring.

In her research, Felicia discovered a "Checklist for Effective Letters" that she found very useful. It is reproduced here so that you can make use of it, too:

A carefully written personalized letter builds goodwill and creates a favorable impression of the writer. . . . To determine whether you have written an effective letter, ask yourself the following questions:

1. <u>Organization</u>. Have you determined the purpose of the letter? Is it to sell, to inform, to persuade, to entertain? Defining the purpose helps you organize your thoughts.

2. <u>Conciseness</u>. Have you used the words and expressions that will best convey your thoughts to the reader? Are only the essential facts included? Information that is irrelevant or too wordy tends to confuse the reader and to reduce comprehension of the message.

3. <u>Clarity</u>. Has your purpose been set forth clearly? Does your choice of words help the reader understand what is being said? Are ideas presented in logical sequence?

4. <u>Completeness</u>. Did you include all the facts, figures, dates, names, and addresses? Are all possible questions answered that might be raised? Stating the facts helps prevent any misunderstandings and helps the reader interpret the message. Insufficient information leaves the reader in doubt and may generate additional correspondence.

5. <u>Tone</u>. Does the tone of your letter indicate friendliness, warmth, and cooperation? The manner in which ideas are conveyed will influence the reader's response.

6. <u>Correctness</u>. Are the dates, facts, and figures correct? Incorrect information may lead to misunderstandings and will necessitate additional communications to clarify the situation.

Reference Manual for Office Workers. Copyright © 1977 by Benziger Bruce & Glencoe, Inc. Material reproduced by permission of the publisher.

Felicia learned about the parts of a business letter (letter elements) and she discovered that there are two basic letter styles (full block and modified block). She also found that there are two methods of punctuating business letters (mixed and open punctuation). Using this knowledge, she wrote a proper business letter proposing that she be awarded a grant to help her pursue her interest in literature.

Following the example of Mr. Coole's letter, Felicia decided to use the modified block style with mixed punctuation. Here is an example of what such a letter looks like:

Letter Element

Modified Block Letter

Letter Element	
Letterhead	JOHNSON CONSTRUCTION 113 Elm Street/Elto, MI 49515 Area Code (616) 761-9363
Date	April 16, 19XX
Inside Address	Mr. John Smith 4113 Murray Street Dayton, OH 45426
Salutation	Dear Mr. Smith:
Body	This is a modified block letter. Every line of the letter begins at the left margin, with the exception of the date and the closing lines, which usually begin at the center of the page. This is one of the more popular letter styles in business because it is easy to set up and gives a balanced appearance. Mixed punctuation means there is a colon after the salutation and a comma after the complimentary closing.
Complimentary Closing	Sincerely yours,
Typed Name Official Title	Mark Peters Office Manager
Reference Initials (initials of the typist)	cs

Jonathan Coole's Letter

ULTRACOM, INC.
1753 Ray Street SE/Grand Rapids, MI 49501
Area Code (616) 371-6200

Jonathan S. Coole
President

March 4, 19XX

Miss Felicia Rodriquez
516 Yost Drive NE
Grand Rapids, MI 49503

Dear Miss Rodriquez:

Thank you for submitting your name to our student grant program. Your interest is appreciated. As you know, we are offering grants of $100 to students in grades six through twelve who have an interest in learning about one of four subject areas: science, mathematics, history, and literature. There will be two grants per subject area for each grade, for a total of 56 grants. Each grant recipient will be expected to spend the money to help further his or her knowledge or understanding of personally chosen topics. I want to encourage you to pursue your interests, and this seems like a good way to do it.

To be eligible for a grant, I want you to send me a business letter explaining your interests and detailing how you would spend the money if it were awarded to you. The ability to write a properly organized business letter will be taken into account in determining who will receive grants.

This program was designed in part to help students develop good communication skills. A number of business leaders and I have joined together to promote the value, usefulness, and *importance* of communication in business. My idea was to have students write letters to apply for grant money. This is how it's done in the real world.

Your letter must be in my office by April 3. That's when our grant board will begin reading them. Remember to clearly state which subject area interests you, and what grade you are in. Good luck, and remember: there are no losers, only winners in this project. Just by participating you are improving yourself.

Yours truly,

Jonathan S. Coole

Jonathan S. Coole
President

tr

Felicia's Grant Proposal Letter

RODRIGUEZ LITERARY ENTERPRISES
516 Yost Drive NE/Grand Rapids, MI 49501
Area Code (616) 555-1538

Felicia M. Rodriguez
President

March 22, 19XX

Mr. Jonathan S. Coole
President
ULTRACOM, Inc.
1753 Ray Street SE
Grand Rapids, MI 49501

Dear Mr. Coole:

I understand that you are offering $100 grants to students with an interest in literature. I am one of those students. I have enjoyed reading all my life, and now I'm beginning to take an interest in the classics. My friends think I'm crazy, but I really enjoy works by authors from the past like Twain, Dickens, Defoe, and Homer. I would like to make a proposal for grant money that will give me a greater opportunity to read and understand what these authors (along with many others) had to say. This will be of great benefit to me in my long term plan of becoming a writer and perhaps a teacher.

1. I would like to take a literature class. This summer the University is offering reading/discussion classes for middle and high school students. There are two sessions I want to attend, ''Mythology'' and ''Humor.'' Cost: $25 per session—Total $50

2. I want to buy my own books. I check lots of books out of the library, but you can't write in them. I want to mark passages and make notes when I read. I also want to have the books around for future reference. Cost: 10 books; $4 per paperback (ave.)—Total $40

3. I need a couple of books about grammar and writing style. This is to help me become a better writer. Cost: 2 books; $5 each—Total $10

This is my proposal. If selected, I will keep receipts for all my expenditures and they will be sent, along with a letter, to the grant board. The letter will document what I did with the money and describe how I benefitted from it.

I want to thank you, Mr. Coole, for supporting those of us who enjoy learning and who *want* to learn (there are lots of us!). I hope that my proposal will earn your serious consideration.

Sincerely yours,

Felicia M. Rodriguez

Felicia M. Rodriguez
Grade: X
Subject: Literature

fr

Name _____ Date _____

CLASSROOM ASSIGNMENT

Widgi-Corp, is a large (fictitious) company that manufactures and distributes widgets. The corporate headquarters is located at 2703 Springwell Avenue, in Los Angeles, California, and the zip code there is 90032. Charles T. Jones is the founder and president of Widgi-Corp. He is a tough but fair businessman, and he is always looking for ways to improve his company.

Read each of the four scenarios below, then choose *one* upon which to base a business letter to Mr. Jones. Use your imagination and be creative as you develop your letter. Don't let your lack of knowledge about widgets keep you from writing about them. *Nobody* knows what a widget is, so for your letter you can have a widget be anything you like.

- You are the chief executive officer of a large company named Hodge Podge Products, Inc., and you need a large quantity of specially-built widgets in a very short amount of time. Write a letter to Mr. Jones explaining the specifics of your problem and asking if he can supply enough widgets in time. Use your own address for Hodge Podge Products, Inc.

- You are a self-employed inventor and you have discovered a way to make widgets work better with a new design and improved materials. Write a letter to Mr. Jones to convince him that he should meet with you and take a look at your ideas.

- You are the head of a business organization and you are looking for a speaker for your national convention. Write to Mr. Jones and ask him to talk about how he made Widgi-Corp. a success in such a short time. You must convince him that speaking to this group will be worth his time and effort.

- Widgi-Corp. needs a new design engineer—a person who is good at coming up with new ideas and thinking of better ways of doing things. Write to Mr. Jones and explain why you are the right person for the job. Give yourself imaginary degrees and job experience to help make a convincing letter.

Name _____   Date _____

ON YOUR OWN

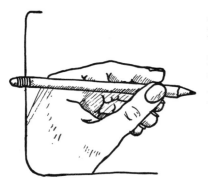

Develop a hypothetical situation in which a business letter must be sent. This situation should come out of your imagination, and it may be as creative as you wish. In the spaces below, explain who is sending what to whom, and why. Then, on separate paper, either write or type the letter that needs to be written.

1. Describe the individual to whom the letter is to be sent and record an *inside address*. Explain what this person does: occupation, job responsibilities, areas of expertise, and so forth. This is to establish a reason for someone to write him or her a letter. Include any information that helps make it clear why the letter is sent to this particular person.

_____

_____

_____

_____

2. Describe the person who is sending the letter, and record the *return address*. Explain specifically why this person is sending his or her letter. In other words, establish a motive for writing the letter.

_____

_____

_____

_____

3. List the points that the person sending the letter wants to make. This will help organize your thoughts before writing the letter. Be as detailed as possible.

_____

_____

_____

_____

_____

_____

_____

ACTIVITY 7.
Composing a Speech

TEACHER PREVIEW

LESSON DESCRIPTIONS

Introductory Narrative ("Good Evening, Ladies and Gentlemen"): Ben explains why he made a speech to the local school board about the fate of a piece of property the board wanted to sell.

Reading Material: Basic information about the reasons for presenting a speech and the components of a good speech, followed by the outline of Ben's presentation and then the text of his speech, "Save Morgan Woods."

Classroom Assignment: Students list three topics about which they feel strongly enough to make a speech. They also identify the makeup of the audience they would prefer for each topic (a speech about homework to an audience of teachers, for example). Ideas for topics and audiences are discussed in class. Then each student selects one topic and records several points that he or she would make in a speech about that topic to a specific audience.

On Your Own: Students use their ideas from the Classroom Assignment as a starting point for outlining and then composing a speech.

SUGGESTIONS FOR SETTING THE STAGE

- Come to class prepared with a written speech about a topic of current concern. Intentionally include common mistakes that people make in speaking, such as biased statements, unsubstantiated conclusions, or inaccuracies. Make specific statements in the speech that can be discussed by students afterward. Have the students pretend they are reporters covering a speech. Their job is to take notes on what you say and call into question anything that doesn't seem right. This can also lead to a class discussion about statements made in the speech: "Point two doesn't seem feasible because . . ." or "I agree with the fourth point because . . ."

Example:

IMPROVING EDUCATION

Members of the class, thank you for allowing me to express my opinions in a speech before you today. I would like to focus on an extremely important and timely question which the adult population discusses endlessly: What can we do to make our educational system better? As we approach the twenty-first century, some things need to be done to improve the quality of education being offered.

Let me give you some details. More students than you can imagine are graduating without the ability to read and write. National test scores show that the United States is falling behind in all subject areas. The drop-out rate has increased alarmingly. Many school districts cannot offer quality programs due to lack of funds. Something must be done to keep our children in school and to ensure that they meet certain requirements before graduating.

Obviously, we can never hope to achieve the high standards that were met in the past, but we can try. I have some concrete, workable solutions which I would like to suggest, and which I will describe briefly:

— Since today's students seem more interested in getting a job than finishing high school, give a diploma to tenth graders who can meet certain requirements and reserve eleventh and twelfth grade for those who really want to learn.

— Allow only those who will complete eleventh and twelfth grade to be involved in school sports.

— Include a community service requirement for all students so that they make a contribution to society in exchange for the free education they're given.

— Increase graduation requirements.

— Bring in people from specialized fields to guest-teach a course or lesson. Give tax breaks to businesses that do this.

— Allow teachers more freedom to create courses; they are professionals and should be educated in college to develop curriculum.

— Hold regular classes Monday through Thursday and have only students who haven't completed assignments or who need extra help come in for school on Fridays. Enrichment classes could also be offered on Friday to students who have done satisfactory work all week.

— Award bonus grades to students whose parents help out at school a certain number of hours per semester.

— Require a higher grade point average to enter college.

— Require foreign language courses in Russian and Japanese.

— As we approach the twenty–first century students should be trained in the following areas: environmental education, economics, current events, computers, global education, geography, communicable diseases, personal finances, democracy, mathematics, science, physical education, fine arts, language arts, career education, emergency medical training, and taxes. Courses in all of these areas should be offered at the high school level.

These are my recommendations for improving education in America. If called upon, I am ready to lead the fight. Remember, young people are our nation's most precious asset. As educators we must do all we can to prepare you for life as adults. Let us be bold in action and not cower before the immensity of the problems. Our educational system must be revised if it is to survive.

• Have a guest speaker come to your class and give a brief speech. This person could be a member of a speech or debate class; it could be a local politician, government official, or teacher; it could be a volunteer parent or professional; or, it could be anyone else who is experienced at speechmaking and willing to donate some time to your class. Follow the speech with a discussion of content and style. Ask students to identify the components, or elements, of a good speech.

• Come to class with the text of a famous speech (or one that is not famous but very well written) and either read it dramatically to the class or invite a guest reader to present it. Discuss the purpose of the speech and its organization. Talk in general about how important some speeches are and about the power of the spoken word.

• Show video tapes of several people making speeches (five-minute clips of each) and compare styles of presentation, including the speakers use of posture, gestures, inflection, vocabulary, emotion, and charisma.

Name _____ Date _____

INTRODUCTORY NARRATIVE

Read the following narrative to learn why Ben made a speech to his local school board.

Good Evening, Ladies and Gentlemen
by Ben

When I heard Morgan Woods was going to be sold, I was surprised and angry. Morgan Woods is like an old friend, and you certainly wouldn't want an old friend to be sold and taken away. I can't imagine seeing the twenty acres of land across the street from my house stripped of its trees and turned into a shopping mall. That would make me and a lot of people I know very sad.

The owner of Morgan Woods is the local board of education, which acquired the land five years ago from the estate of a man who made his fortune in real estate here in our town. In his will he said he owed the school district something for the fine education he had received as a child, and so he was repaying the debt by giving the board the woods, to do with as it pleased. He said that, in its wisdom, the board could decide how to use the land. What the board decided to do, after five years of inaction, was to sell Morgan Woods to a development company and use the money to set up a grant program for teachers.

I heard about the proposal to sell Morgan Woods when it was announced that there would be a special meeting, open to the public, at which all points of view would be discussed. Various interest groups were asked to send representatives to the meeting to present their opinions to the board. It seemed to me that students should be represented too, so I wrote a letter asking that I be allowed to make a speech at the meeting, to give the students' point of view. To my surprise, a few days later I received a letter from the board inviting me to come to the meeting. It said that I had been put on the meeting's agenda, and that I would have ten minutes to make my case.

Well, after a lot of work writing and practicing, I went to the meeting and made my speech, along with quite a few other people. I don't know if I had anything to do with it, but the board, at its next regular meeting, voted not to sell the land! Morgan Woods has been saved! It hasn't been decided what *will* be done with the land, but the idea of selling it to a shopping mall developer has been dropped. I am very pleased with this decision and I am proud of myself for contributing to the debate. I learned a lot from my experience of making a speech to the board of education, and I know that the next time I have to make a speech it will be a lot easier. Composing and presenting a speech is not as easy as I thought it would be (I was *nervous* standing in front of those people!), but it sure is a good thing to know how to do.

Name _____ Date _____

READING MATERIAL

Making a speech to an audience of interested listeners provides an opportunity to present your ideas, opinions, knowledge, and experiences to others. Usually a speech is designed to persuade, teach, or motivate people. When you make a speech you are expressing your thoughts publicly, in an effort to influence how other people think or behave. To be successful, a speech must be carefully composed before it is presented. Presentation style is important, but so is content. In order to be persuaded, taught, or motivated, an audience wants to hear a well organized, thoughtful, accurate speech. Such a speech comes from careful composition, which is what this lesson is all about.

Most speeches have three parts: introduction, organized presentation of information, and conclusion. The introduction recognizes the people to whom the speech is being made, provides a few autobiographical details about the speaker, and "breaks the ice" with a brief story or joke or statement that makes the audience feel comfortable and ready to hear more. The main body of the speech presents whatever ideas and opinions the speaker wishes to impress upon the minds of his or her listeners. To make a lasting impression, the speech should flow easily from one point to the next. The conclusion summarizes the speech in a simple statement (when people remember *it,* they will recall other parts of the speech as well), thanks the sponsoring group for asking the speaker to talk, encourages the audience to think about the points that have been made, and bids everyone a good evening (or morning or afternoon).

A good way to begin composing a speech is to outline the points that you want to make. Ben wrote his speech by first collecting information, then putting his opinions, together with the information he had gathered, into an outline, and finally writing the speech in paragraphs. Here is Ben's outline, followed by his speech:

Save Morgan Woods (Outline)

I. Introduction
    A. Thank superintendent Johnson and board members for letting me talk
    B. Explain who I am
    C. Tell the story of ''Trash Day, U.S.A.''
    D. Explain that the story is an example of why Morgan Woods should not be destroyed, but there are many other good reasons . . .
II. Points to make
    A. Students cut through the woods to get to school. If they have to walk around the block, sidewalks will have to be built.
    B. The board itself might need the land some day: population in the area is increasing, which is why they want to build a mall. A new school might be necessary.
    C. Morgan Woods would be a great place for environmental studies and nature trails.
    D. Animals live in Morgan Woods; they need a home.
    E. Children need a place like Morgan Woods to play; it's good for

READING MATERIAL, CONT'D

```
            them. Maybe the schools and the city can work together to make
            it a park.
    III. Conclusion
        A. If you get cash for the land you can invest it and use the
           interest money for teacher grants. Please consider the
           possibility that keeping Morgan Woods is also an investment in
           the future.
        B. I ask you to take the points from this speech into
           consideration when you decide the fate of Morgan Woods.
        C. Thank you again for the chance to speak.
        D. Good night.
```

Save Morgan Woods (Speech)

(Superintendent Johnson introduces Ben as the next speaker.)

Thank you Superintendent Johnson. Good evening, ladies and gentlemen of the school board, and thank you for allowing me to speak to you tonight. My name is Ben Otten and I live on Maple Street, right across from Morgan Woods. I have lived there all my life. I go to school at Jefferson Junior/Senior High, and I am a member of the student council. My interest in Morgan Woods comes from spending my whole life walking and playing there.

It's hard to explain why a place where all you do is play or explore or walk is more valuable than money. Let me tell you about last year's "Trash Day, U.S.A.," and maybe that will help show what Morgan Woods means to people. Over 100 people came to spend a day cleaning up the woods. They spent the entire day combing every square inch. I heard parents telling children about adventures in the woods during *their* childhood. One father and mother climbed a tree with their daughter, "just like when they were kids." My dad and I worked together all day. He told me stories about when he was young, and he told me that my grandpa played in Morgan Woods, too. As we hauled away bags of paper, cans, and other trash, it made us both feel good to be taking care of the woods, and all those other people felt the same way. I see several people here tonight who participated in "Trash Day, U.S.A." All we want is for you to understand how important Morgan Woods is to us.

The love of people for Morgan Woods is one good reason for not destroying it. There are others. For example, has anyone considered how children who normally walk through the woods on their way to school will get there once construction on a mall begins? There are no sidewalks in our neighborhood, and students have traditionally walked a diagonal trail through the woods to the corner of Spring Street and Michigan Avenue, where sidewalks begin. If you sell the land, at least 2,000 feet of sidewalk will have to be poured, or there will be many students walking on the shoulders of two very busy streets.

Another reason for not selling the land is that you might need it some day. The population in our part of the city is increasing. Houses and apartments are being built all over the place, and new businesses are being started. That's why some people want to build a mall over there. But new people mean more students, and the schools are already full. You're probably going to have to build a new school some day, so why not do it in the midst of a woods on land you already own?

There are things that could be done with Morgan Woods. It would be a great place for an environmental study program, especially if a school is eventually built there. Nature trails could be built, special varieties of trees, flowers, and shrubs could be planted, identification

READING MATERIAL, CONT'D

guides could be developed, and feeding stations for birds and small mammals could be set up. The land could also be used for overnight camping by school groups. Finally, biology classes could use the woods as an outdoor laboratory, for observing and experimenting with nature.

I don't want you to forget that there are thousands of animals in Morgan Woods. They need a home, and I hate to think of them running across Illinois Avenue to get away from a bulldozer. It would be much better to study them than to evict them.

My last point is an important one: children need a place like Morgan Woods to play. Playing outside is *good* for kids, and the next nearest place, which is just a small park, is fifteen blocks away. Maybe you could work with the city to make the woods into a park with improved walking trails, exercise areas, drinking fountains, playground equipment, picnic areas, and so forth. All of the young and the young at heart would appreciate that kind of arrangement.

Let me sum up with this final thought. It is obvious that if you get cash for the land you can invest it and use the interest money for teacher grants, and I'm not saying that's bad. But *keeping* Morgan Woods is also a sensible investment. Every person in the community, not just current students, will benefit from having such a beautiful piece of land available for recreation, and the school district may *need* the land for future expansion, or for additional educational programs. Before you make your final decision about the fate of Morgan Woods, please take the points from this speech into consideration.

I want to thank you once again for inviting me to make a presentation at tonight's meeting. I appreciate the chance to speak my mind. Good night.

Name _____   Date _____

CLASSROOM ASSIGNMENT

There are many topics about which students your age have strong opinions. If an appropriate audience were available, you could undoubtedly think of things you'd like to say. For example, suppose you could have the parents of everyone in your school in an auditorium, and you could tell them whatever you wanted. What would it be? What message would you like to deliver to your parents, and those of your friends and classmates? Or suppose it could be arranged to have all the teachers in your school district listen seriously and with completely open minds to a speech from you. What would you tell them?

On the lines below, record three topics that are important enough to make a speech about. Next to each topic, indicate who you would like to have in the audience (examples: teachers, parents, coaches, doctors, movie makers, drunk drivers, couch potatoes, dropouts, or the president and his cabinet).

Topic   Audience

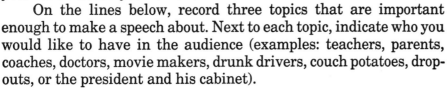

_____   _____

_____   _____

_____   _____

Be prepared to discuss your topic and audience ideas as the class develops a list of topics and issues that would be worth speaking out about. Choose one (it can be one of your original ideas, or you can use one of the others from the discussion), and write three points that you would bring up if you were to give the speech. Your points should be written in complete sentences.

Topic: _____

Audience: _____

Point 1: _____

_____

_____

Point 2: _____

_____

_____

Point 3: _____

_____

_____

Name _____ Date _____

ON YOUR OWN

Using the information from your Classroom Assignment as a starting point, outline a speech and then write it in paragraph form. Put your outline on this sheet. It should be as neat and complete as possible, because you will turn it in for approval before composing your speech. Make a rough draft outline on a separate piece of paper before recording your final outline here.

Your teacher will check to be sure that you have a solid basis for writing a speech, including good arguments, continuity of ideas, and proper organization. When you get the outline back, begin composing a speech, taking your teacher's comments into account.

_____

_____ Outline is approved
_____ Outline needs more work; resubmit on _____

_____

ACTIVITY 8.
Interviewing an Adult

TEACHER PREVIEW

LESSON DESCRIPTIONS

Introductory Narrative ("May I Ask a Few Questions?"): Julie describes her interest in journalism and explains why she decided to interview her grandmother.

Reading Material: An explanation of why interviewing skills are important to develop and a list of things to do to prepare for conducting an interview, followed by a transcript of Julie's interview with her grandma. The transcript can be the basis for a class discussion about a number of topics that Julie and her grandma talk about.

Classroom Assignment: Students interview an adult in a "press conference" setting in which they raise their hands, individuals are called upon to ask questions, and everyone records the answers. The person being interviewed should be a guest speaker: a local politician, a parent volunteer, the building principal, a government worker, a professional (doctor, lawyer, engineer), a college professor, or anyone else that might be an interesting subject for an interview. Students are told ahead of time whom they will be interviewing, and they come to class prepared with questions to ask. From their notes, students write summaries of the interview, as if they were writing news reports of a press conference.

On Your Own: Students prepare for an interview with an adult by writing letters requesting an appointment, making lists of appropriate questions, obtaining a tape recorder (if possible), and actually conducting an interview. Then they either prepare a transcript of the interview or make an outline and write a summary of it.

SUGGESTIONS FOR SETTING THE STAGE

• Have a discussion about interviewing someone who was born in 1920: what kinds of things would you be able to ask about? What has this person seen happen in the course of his or her lifetime? As a class, develop a time line from 1920 to the present, including major historical, social, and scientific events. For example, the Great Depression, World War Two, polio vaccine, computers, space flight, television, Vietnam, air travel, and a host of other things would appear on such a time line. Talk about how interesting it would be to have a first-hand account from someone who saw these things happen or develop, for example, someone who has a "before-and-after" perspective on television.

- Bring videotaped segments of televised interviews from morning news programs, news magazines, news conferences, and the like. Analyze the tapes for interviewing techniques. Have students record the questions in writing as they watch the segments. Talk about how they were phrased and delivered. Did the interviewer get the intended answer? Did he or she have to probe more deeply, or ask more pointed questions? Was the interview well done? Remember, just because it's televised doesn't mean it's well done.

- Tell the students that they can interview anyone in the world that they want; each student gets his or her choice. Have them write at the top of a piece of paper their own name and the name of the person they want to interview. Then they should record five questions they want to ask in the interview. These may be funny or ridiculous, but it introduces the idea of interviewing quite nicely. Have students share their questions with the class.

Name _____ Date _____

INTRODUCTORY NARRATIVE

Read the following narrative to find out why Julie wanted to learn how to interview an adult.

May I Ask a Few Questions?
by Julie

My interest in journalism dates back quite a few years. I am told that when I was little I would watch my older brothers play and then come into the living room, put my hands behind my back, and tell my parents what "the boys" were up to. I wasn't tattling, I was reporting. I've been that way all my life. It's like I have an irresistible urge to describe to others what I've seen or experienced. I keep scrapbooks of vacations, and I record the things I see and do on special occasions in journals. Then, when I can get someone to listen to me I report the important details as factually as possible.

A lot of times I do this jokingly. For example, I might say to a group of family friends, "This is Julie Newberg, in the Newberg living room, with an up-to-date report on the latest Newberg family outing. In this report I will show, using photographs, maps, and perhaps a live interview, just how much fun a family can have during a weekend at Pine Valley Amusement Park. I will also describe a near disaster when one family member became dramatically ill midway through a ride on the *Shrieking Dragon* roller coaster. Fortunately, the illness was brief." People seem to enjoy my reports, or at least they humor me by pretending that they do.

Now that I'm older, I'm becoming more serious about learning to be a journalist. When I was in the sixth grade, I started an imaginary magazine, and I still write articles and editorials for it. It's imaginary because it's not published, but it's also very real because I actually write material for it. I try to complete one issue per year by writing a piece every eight or nine weeks. Each "magazine" consists of five or six articles and an editorial. It's a way for me to write about what's on my mind.

This year I started out with a sports feature, focusing on our girls' basketball team. When I finished that piece, I began looking for something more challenging to write about, and that's when it occurred to me that I should learn how to interview an adult. I decided to choose an interesting adult, conduct an interview, record what was said on tape, make a transcript of the conversation, and write an article entitled "A Talk With _____ ."

I chose as a subject one of my favorite people, my Grandma Newberg. I sent her a formal letter explaining my project and requesting an appointment for an interview. She promptly responded, granting my request and setting a time during Thanksgiving weekend for me to interview her. My family went to her house for three days, and it was the perfect time for us to be alone for a couple of hours.

My interview with Grandma Newberg was fascinating. I got to know her better than I had before, and she gave me enough material for a really good article. I also learned a lot about asking questions in an interview situation. All in all, I'd say it was a valuable experience for both of us, and it certainly added to my journalistic skills. I think my next interview assignment will be with an adult I don't know. I feel ready to do that now.

Name _____ Date _____

READING MATERIAL

Interviewing an adult can be a truly interesting experience. You can learn a lot from adults, especially if they think you are serious about getting answers to your questions. There are countless reasons for interviewing an adult, from asking for advice about school and career choices or seeking information about a hobby to digging into your family history or simply finding out more about a particular person. Whatever the reason, you will get more out of your interview if you know what you're doing.

There are several basic rules or guidelines that should be kept in mind as you prepare for an interview. These are the steps Julie followed for her interview with her grandma.

- Determine a reason for conducting an interview.
- Decide which person you want to interview.
- Write a letter to (or call) the person and make an appointment. Do this even if it is a relative or close friend that you want to interview.
- Make a list of questions that you want to ask.
- Take a tape recorder to the interview if at all possible. If it is *not* possible, be prepared to take rapid and accurate notes. You should take some notes even if you do have a tape recorder, so that a bad tape won't be a disaster.
- Transcribe the tape (or rewrite your notes) into a written record of the interview.
- Use the information from the interview in whatever way you wish.

Below is Julie's transcribed interview with her grandma. Notice how she followed some of her original questions up with second and third questions to help clarify things her grandma said. This is a very important technique for an interviewer.

A Talk with Grandma Newberg

Julie: Thanks for doing this with me, Grandma. I'm praticing to be a reporter, so I'm going to pretend that you are a famous person and that I don't even know you. Do you mind doing it that way?

Grandma Newberg: Not at all, Julie. I think it sounds like fun.

J: Let me start with some general questions about your life. Where were you born, where did you go to school, where did you live, and so forth.

GN: Well I was born just down the road from here, in a little town called Ashley. The house where I was born is still there. I lived in that house until I was married. I took classes at Ashley school, which was a little two-room schoolhouse. I went there through the eighth grade, then I went to Washington High School in Taylorville.

J: What do you remember about life in those days that would be of interest to my readers?

GN: Oh, dear; I have lots and lots of memories. I remember all the children running out of their houses to watch the train rumble through town. And I remember the town's Fourth of July picnics. That's where I first met your grandfather Newberg. He was playing softball and got hit on the head by a fly ball. He was so embarrassed! I offered him a

READING MATERIAL, CONT'D

towel with ice to put on the bruise. He ate his picnic lunch with me, that led to our first date, and we were married several years later. Those were happy times.

J: So you had a happy childhood?

GN: I seem to remember the happy times more easily, but really life was hard most of the time. You see, Julie, I lived most of my teen years during the Great Depression, and our family was very poor. We had food, clothing, and shelter, but little more. And my father, your great grandpa Stewart, worked twelve and fifteen hour days on Wilson's dairy farm to earn a dollar a day. I didn't have pretty dresses or many toys. For Christmas each of us children received one piece of warm clothing, and we were grateful for it. Cornbread and navy beans were a staple of our diet. But were we happy? Yes, I guess we were, because we had each other, and everyone else was in the same boat. We appreciated and enjoyed the simple things in life, and I don't think people do that so much any more.

J: What jobs have you held in your life?

GN: I worked as a waitress when I was in high school, for a few hours each evening. That was the only job available to a teenage girl at the time, and I was lucky to get it. I worked for almost nothing. During the early 1940s I worked in a factory that made blankets. First I was an edge stitcher, then I was an inspector. Your grandfather and I were married in 1945, and for ten years I stayed home and had children. Then I decided to be a school teacher and started taking night classes. When my youngest son, your uncle Bob, started school, I began full-time classes and got my degree. Then I taught fourth grade for twenty-five years before retiring.

J: You said you worked in a blanket factory. Was that around here?

GN: Yes. It was where Maple Lanes Bowling Alley is now, the same building. We made blankets for the military. When World War II was over, the demand for blankets went down and they closed the factory.

J: What is the most exciting thing that has ever happened to you?

GN: Without a doubt, it was graduating from college. It was the most exciting because I think it is the greatest accomplishment of my life. I was told I shouldn't do it and that I *couldn't* do it. I proved something very important to myself by graduating from college.

J: What was that? I mean, what did you prove?

GN: That a woman with a family could start late and still have a career.

J: What is one important thing that you've learned in your life?

GN: Patience is the greatest virtue.

J: I don't understand.

GN: What I mean is, most things of value take time to develop, and that includes success and a feeling of fulfillment in your life. Patience is the ability to wait. But it is also the willingness to take whatever steps are necessary to do something *right* so it will have lasting value. Whether we're talking about relationships between men and women, career goals, raising families, earning good grades, or whatever, I've learned that patience will serve you well.

J: What is the most amazing thing you've ever seen?

GN: The most amazing thing? Someone your age can't realize how difficult that question is for someone my age. In my life truly unbelievable things have happened. I guess I'd have to say that seeing a man walk on the moon is the most amazing, because when I was a girl it would have required magic to do it. When I was a little girl, many people were still getting around in horse and buggies, and airplanes were rarely seen. Space travel was simply impossible; unthinkable; unimaginable. From buggies to the moon is a long way to come in one person's lifetime.

J: OK, let me change directions and ask you, what was the saddest time in your life?

READING MATERIAL, CONT'D

GN: Well, the very saddest time is one I'll never fully get over, and that is the death of your grandpa Newberg. It happened so suddenly and unexpectedly that I, well, I felt like a part of me just vaporized. It's lonely without him, but life goes on and I'm enjoying the rest of my family as much as is humanly possible.

The next saddest time is one from which I am completely recovered. That was when your dad returned from the Vietnam War. He was changed; dramatically changed. He was reclusive—just wanted to be alone, and stopped getting together with his friends. I was very worried about him. Then he went to college like he'd planned to do three years earlier, and he met your mom. The night he introduced her to me he had his old smile and I stopped being worried. He was changed, but he was OK, and that gave me a great sense of relief.

J: One last question before wrapping up this interview. If you could offer one piece of advice to people my age, what would it be?

GN: Be ready for change. The only certain thing about this world is that it will change, so be ready for it. I've seen enough in my life to know for sure that things can happen very quickly, both for the good and for the bad. People who are ready to adjust to new situations and who can adapt to changing conditions will always have an advantage over people who don't think about such things. Never assume that the world will remain the same; I can guarantee that it *won't*.

J: Thank you, Grandma Newberg, for spending this time with me.

GN: You're very welcome, Julie. I enjoyed it more than you will ever know.

Name ——————————————— Date ———————————————

CLASSROOM ASSIGNMENT

During our next class you will interview an adult in a "press conference" setting, where members of the class ask questions and the person being questioned provides answers. You will take notes and from your notes you will make a written summary of the interview. Here is the assignment:

Name of the person being interviewed: ———————————————————

Position, occupation, or area of expertise: ——————————————————

——

Additional information about this person: ——————————————————

——

——

- Record at least five questions that you would like to ask this person.

——

——

——

——

- Plan to participate during the questioning period. Your teacher may call on individuals even if they don't raise their hands, so be prepared with a question if called upon.
- Each person will take notes on all of the questions and answers. Be ready to write fast, because the person being interviewed should not be requested to repeat answers unless they are unclear.
- From your notes, write a summary of the interview. Be as complete and thorough as possible; look upon this assignment as if you were a reporter writing about a news conference.

Name _____ Date _____

ON YOUR OWN

Choose an adult family member (parent, grandparent, aunt, uncle), or an adult friend, and set up a time for an interview. Put your request into the form of a letter and state specifically why you want the interview. Go to the interview prepared with a set of questions that you would like to have answered and be ready to follow up with more specific questions if you don't get clear answers. If possible, record your interview on tape.

Here is the assignment:

   I. In the space below (and on the back of this sheet, if necessary) write one paragraph that explains why you want to interview the person you have chosen. What do you expect to learn, or gain, or understand as a result of the interview? You may be asked to hand your paragraph in before proceeding with Part II. **Due date:** _____

  II. Write a letter to the person you have chosen, requesting an interview. Use the paragraph from Part I as a guide for the body of the letter. Explain why you want the interview and ask for a convenient time. You may be asked to hand your letter in before sending or delivering it. **Due date** _____

 III. Make a list of questions to use during the interview. Be sure your questions require a response, and not just a "yes" or "no" answer. Prepare at least five good questions, and yes, you may be asked to hand your questions in before conducting your interview. **Due date:** _____

  IV. Conduct the interview, and tape record it if you can. After the interview, you may choose *one* of these two assignment options:

   A. Prepare a transcript of the interview. In other words, write down what was said, the questions and answers.

   B. Make an outline of the main points and then write a summary of the interview.

   V. Your transcript or outline and summary will be handed in. **Due date:** _____

© 1990 by The Center for Applied Research in Education

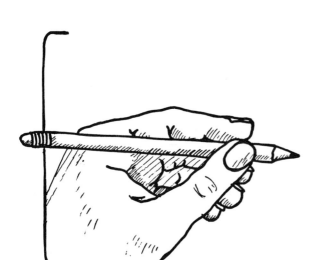

ACTIVITY 9.
Recording Information on Notecards

TEACHER PREVIEW

LESSON DESCRIPTIONS

Introductory Narrative ("Bits and Pieces"): Anthony tells about learning to conduct a research project by recording facts on notecards. He then explains why this skill became valuable when he was assigned a research project in science.

Reading Material: An explanation of how notecards can help a person write reports in his or her own words, followed by a format for organizing notecards and bibliography cards. Also included is a sample of the notecards and bibliography cards Anthony made for his report on the sun. These can be used as a model for students.

Classroom Assignment: Students conduct an information search in the school library, or in a classroom "mini-library," to find facts about specific topics. Each student has a different topic, which is taken from the list provided on the Classroom Assignment Sheet. The recommended way to assign topics is to write them on slips of paper or notecards and have each student draw one out of a box or hat. This blind draw is likely to take students to areas of the library they haven't explored, looking for information about subjects they would not have chosen for themselves. If they can find books about randomly chosen topics, they can locate information about virtually anything. The assignment calls for students to make notecards and bibliography cards, to be turned in at the end of the class period.

On Your Own: Students choose topics, conduct research, record facts on notecards, prepare bibliography cards, and write short reports. Topics are chosen from the list on the Classroom Assignment Sheet. Students may choose a different topic with your approval. Working independently, each student finds at least three sources of information, records at least twenty facts on notecards, and makes a bibliography card for each source. These are handed in with the report.

SUGGESTIONS FOR SETTING THE STAGE

- Conduct a preliminary "information search" (in preparation for the Classroom Assignment) to ensure that students know how to use the library. Record the topics from the Classroom Assignment Sheet on individual notecards and take the class to the library. Have each student draw one card, find a book about that topic, and record the publisher, date of publication, and city of publication on a notecard. Then he or she brings the book and card to you (or a librarian or aide), and if it's an acceptable book and the information on the card is accurate, the student earns a point (or a check mark on a class roster) and draws another topic card to start the process over again. The information asked for is sometimes difficult to find, and this activity will help students learn where to look when they make bibliography cards later on.

- Have the entire class make a practice set of notecards to help them understand the format used in this activity. Examples are provided in the Reading Material of this activity. Prepare a set of notecards about a topic currently being covered in the curriculum. For example, take three simple, brief facts from each of three different books (nine notecards altogether) about a topic from the social studies or history text book. Make a bibliography card for each book. Bring the books and your set of cards to class. Give each student twelve blank notecards, and take them through this exercise (using the Civil War as an example). Tell them:

1. "Record the subject in the center of the top line. The subject is 'Social Studies.' Write 'Social Studies' on the top line of all twelve cards.

2. "On the left side of the next line record the topic being studied. The topic is the Civil War. Write 'Civil War' on the second line of all twelve cards.

3. "Now set three cards to the side. These will be bibliography cards.

4. "On the right side of the second line ('Civil War' is written on the left side) write 'card ____' and number the nine notecards 1–9.

5. "On the left side of the bottom line of each notecard write 'pg ____.' Each time a fact is recorded, the page from which it came should also be recorded at the lower left of the notecard.

6. "On the right side of the bottom line of each notecard write 'see bib. card ____.' A bibliography card should be made for each source used in a project. Every notecard from a single source should have the same bibliography card number in this space.

7. "Now take the three bibliography cards and on the right side of the second line write 'bib. card ____.' Number them 1–3.

8. "Fill out the bibliography card as you go through the facts from each source."

Each student now has a set of properly organized notecards. Continue the lesson by providing information to be recorded:

9. Hold up one book and tell students that the first three facts were taken from it.

10. Read the first fact as the class records it on "card 1," then record the page on which it was found and the bib. card number (1).

11. Read each succeeding fact, recording page numbers and bib. card numbers.

12. After all the facts from the first source are recorded, fill out bib. card no. 1, and then proceed with facts from book number 2.

13. Continue this process until everyone in the class has a set of nine notecards and three bibliography cards that is identical to the one you brought to class.

Name _____   Date _____

INTRODUCTORY NARRATIVE

Read the following narrative to discover how Anthony used his knowledge of notecards and bibliographies to complete a difficult science project.

Bits and Pieces
by Anthony

When Mr. Highsmith told us we were going to learn research skills, beginning with notecards and bibliographies, my friends and I all sighed and rolled our eyes toward the ceiling. We didn't really see any reason to learn that stuff. I mean, we figured that it's boring and we'll never use it again, so why learn it? It seemed like a waste of time, and we all felt that we had better things to do. Mr. Highsmith must have noticed our reaction (some of the sighs were more like groans) because he started off by reminding us in his humorously blunt manner that we really had no choice in the matter, so why not lighten up and listen to what he had to say?

Mr. Highsmith is a good English teacher. He constantly places emphasis on being successful in the twenty-first century. Change, he says, is one of the few things we can be sure of, so we should prepare ourselves to deal with it. That is almost an exact quote of something he says at *least* two or three times a week. Anyway, in defense of his decision to teach us about notecards and bibliographies, he told us that one of our future needs will be the ability to find, record, organize, and present information. Learning to find information and make a set of notecards lays the foundation for independent learning. It provides a way of recording individual facts so that they can be arranged, rearranged, and *used.*

We learned a system for making notecards and bibliographies from Mr. Highsmith that will be useful any time we need to do research. He told us new computer programs for information gathering follow basically the same procedure as the one he taught us. When we see such programs in future careers, or college, we will be prepared to use them.

Recently I learned just how valuable my research skills could be. Three weeks ago Mrs. Pierce, my science teacher, assigned a research project to everyone in her physical science classes. We could choose our own topics from one of the following areas: geology, chemistry, physics, meteorology, or astronomy. I decided to study the area of astronomy and I chose the sun as my topic.

You could tell right away that students who had taken Mr. Highsmith's class knew how to get started and what to do, while this was difficult for many of the others. It was a big advantage to already have the basic skills for doing an independent research assignment. I was able to head right for the library to begin my project while some of my friends struggled with simple questions like: How do you find information in the library? What is a bibliography? How do you organize information for a report? How do you choose a topic? I knew the answers to these questions, which allowed me to do the project properly and mostly on my own. To the amazement of everyone who has ever known me, I turned it in ahead of time and got an A−, proving that being prepared really does make a difference.

Name ————————————————— Date —————————————————

READING MATERIAL

Have you ever had a teacher insist that you write a report "in your own words?" Did you find such an assignment a difficult task? Using notecards can make the job easier. By recording one simple or concise fact on each card you are making it possible to get away from copying information word for word straight from a book or encyclopedia. You can organize a set of notecards so that similar facts are grouped together, even if they came from several different books. Each group of cards represents a paragraph in the report. The paragraphs will be written in your own words because facts from a variety of sources are being combined. If the report is to be smooth and easy to read, you must connect the facts in a logical order with sentences that describe, explain, question, compare, or contrast. Make your report *interesting* by using your own thoughts, ideas, and impressions to introduce and discuss the facts you've found.

Notecards are a very useful tool. They let you manipulate information by moving facts around on a desk top. This is a good way to decide how best to organize the facts that have been collected. Once they have been organized and grouped, the report can be written.

The following pages show some of Anthony's notecards on the sun. Examples of his bibliography cards are also provided. Look them over carefully to see how he was taught to arrange his cards and record information on them. Remember that an accurate bibliography is *very* important. These are things you should keep in mind:

Notecards

- The **subject** being studied (astronomy, Civil War, famous authors, and so forth) goes in the center of the top line.
- The **topic** you are studying independently (Mars, The Battle of Gettysburg, Mark Twain, and so forth) goes on the *left* side of the next line (or you may skip a line).
- The **card number** goes on the *right* side of the same line. Notecards are numbered consecutively, starting with card 1.
- A **fact** goes in the body of each card.
- The **page number** of the book in which the fact was found goes on the left side of the bottom line.
- The **number of the bibliography card** telling which source the fact came from goes on the right side of the bottom line.
- Your **name** goes on the back of each notecard.

Bibliography Cards

- The **subject** being studied goes on the top line.
- The **topic** you are studying independently goes on the left side of the next line.
- The **bibliography card number** ("bib. card no.") goes on the right side of the same line.
- Information about one source goes in the body of each card.

READING MATERIAL, CONT'D

Notecards from Anthony's Project on the Sun

Astronomy	Astronomy
The Sun Card no. 1	The Sun Card no. 2
Stars are huge balls of hot gases; their energy comes from fusion.	Fusion is when atoms of hydrogen combine, or fuse, to form helium.
pg: 7 See bib. card no. 1	pg: 7 See bib. card no. 1
Astronomy	Astronomy
The Sun Card no. 3	The Sun Card no. 4
The Sun is one of 500 billion stars in our galaxy: the Milky Way.	100 Earths could be lined up across the middle of the Sun.
pg: 11 See bib. card no. 1	pg: 7 See bib. card no. 1
Astronomy	Astronomy
The Sun Card no. 5	The Sun Card no. 6
The Sun is the nearest star to the Earth: it is about 93,000,000 miles away.	The Sun was "born" about 5 billion years ago.
pg: 7 See bib. card no. 1	pg: 1 See bib. card no. 2
Astronomy	Astronomy
The Sun Card no. 7	The Sun Card no. 8
The Sun weighs more than 300,000 planets like Earth.	The Sun weighs 2.2 billion billion billion tons.
pg: 2 See bib. card no. 2	pg: 2 See bib. card no. 2

© 1990 by The Center for Applied Research in Education

READING MATERIAL, CONT'D

Notecards and Bibliography Cards from Anthony's Project on the Sun

---

Astronomy

The Sun   Card no. 9

Each second the Sun loses 4.5 million tons of its mass by converting it to energy.

pg: 12   See bib. card no. 2

Astronomy

The Sun   Card no. 10

Temperatures inside the Sun reach 16 million degrees Celsius.

pg: 7   See bib. card no. 2

Astronomy

The Sun   Card no. 11

The Sun's diameter is 864,000 miles.

pg: 66   See bib. card no. 3

Astronomy

The Sun   Card no. 12

The Earth's orbit around the Sun is an ellipse.

pg: 66   See bib. card no. 3

Astronomy

The Sun   Bib. card no. 1
Author: Gallant, Roy A.
Title: The Macmillan Book of Astronomy
City: New York
Date: 1986
Publisher: Macmillan Publishing Co.
Page: 7

Astronomy

The Sun   Bib. Card No. 2
Author: McAleer, Neil
Title: The Cosmic Mind-Boggling Book
City: New York
Date: 1982
Publisher: Warner Books, Inc.
Pages: 1,2,4,7

Astronomy

The Sun   Bib. card no. 3
Author: Mayall, Newton R., Margaret Mayall, and Jerome Wyckoff
Title: The Sky Observer's Guide
City: New York
Date: 1985
Publisher: Western Publishing Co., Inc.
Page: 66

Name ————————————————— Date ——————————————

CLASSROOM ASSIGNMENT

This activity is called an information search. Working either in the school library or from a mini-library in your classroom, find information about one of the topics below and make a set of notecards about it. Since you have only one class period in which to complete the assignment, your set of notecards will be rather small. The purpose of the activity is to see if you can locate facts and record them properly; you do not have to collect enough information for a report.

You will either choose a topic or draw a slip of paper (from a box or hat) with a topic written on it.
Record your topic here: ————————————————————————
Follow these steps to complete the assignment:

- Find at least three books that contain information about your topic. Only *one* of these books may be an encyclopedia.
- Record facts from the books on notecards. Make at least three notecards for each book. Each fact should be brief and easy to understand, and each notecard should be properly organized. Use the samples of Anthony's notecards as a model.
- Make a bibliography card for each book you use. The On Your Own activity includes information about making bibliographies for books and encyclopedias, as well as for periodicals and newspapers.
- At the end of the period, hand in *at least*:
    * nine notecards (three from each book)
    * three bibliography cards.
- Be sure your name is on the back of each card.

Topics for the Information Search

Airplanes	Empires	Military
Ancient civilizations	Explorers	Music
Astronomy	Fish	Nuclear power
Automobiles	Flowers	The Olympics
Baseball	Forts	Pilgrims
Basketball	Football	Pioneers
Birds	Fungi	Prehistory
Body systems	Geology	Presidents
Cities	Government	Reptiles
Coins and money	Health	Rockets
Computers	Houseplants	Sculpture
Countries	Native Americans	Ships and boats
Crusades	Insects	Spiders
Dance	Inventions	Stamps
Dinosaurs	Invertebrates	Television
Economics	Mammals	Trains and railroads
Electricity	Medicine	Trees

Name ———————————————— Date ————————————————

ON YOUR OWN

Choose a topic from the list provided on the Classroom Assignment Sheet and conduct an independent research project. Collect enough information on notecards to write a short report (two or three pages) about the topic you have chosen. It is a good idea to focus on a specific aspect of the topic. For example, if you select "body systems," you should narrow your project to respiration, circulation, digestion, or one of the other systems of the body. You may choose a topic that is not on the list with your teacher's approval.

The topic I have chosen to study is ————————————————————

I will focus on this aspect of my topic: ————————————————————

Prepare a set of notecards and bibliography cards, similar to the one developed by Anthony, about the topic you have chosen to study. Then write a short research report and turn in both the report and the set of cards. Here are the minimum requirements:

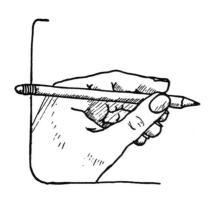

- Locate at least three sources of information about the topic and prepare a properly made bibliography card for each. Only one of these sources may be an encyclopedia.
- Record at least twenty facts on properly organized notecards. Be sure to include a page number and a bibliography card reference on each notecard.
- Arrange the notecards in the best order for a report on the topic.
- Write a two- to three-page report.
- Turn in the report along with the set of notecards and bibliography cards.

Book	*Encyclopedia*
Author, last name first	Author, last name first
Full title, underlined	Title of article, in quotes
Place of publication	Name of encyclopedia, underlined
Date of publication	Date of publication in parentheses
Publisher	Volume number (or letter)
Page(s)	Page(s)
Library call no.	

Periodicals	*Newspapers*
Author, last name first	Author, last name first
Article title, in quotes	Article title, in quotes
Name of periodical, underlined	Name of paper, underlined
Volume number	Date
Date, in parentheses	Section
Page(s)	Page(s)

ACTIVITY 10.
Describing a News Event

TEACHER PREVIEW

LESSON DESCRIPTIONS

Introductory Narrative ("Tell It Like It Is"): John explains how he botched an effort to write an article about a robbery that he witnessed by not following good journalistic methods. He also offers a brief, revised article that gives all of the facts clearly and accurately.

Reading Material: A review of the five *W*s, along with a list of seven points to keep in mind when writing a newspaper article or when reporting in any manner about an event. This is followed by John's first article describing the robbery he witnessed. Encourage students to think about why this article is poorly written, and discuss their ideas in class.

Classroom Assignment: PREPARATION REQUIRED Students view a short (no more than ten minutes) portion of a videotape showing some type of action. Then each student records what was on the tape by listing the sequence of action as accurately as possible. After fifteen or twenty minutes students are put in small groups and each group composes a final version of what its members saw. During the next class period, each small group presents its version to the class. After the presentations are completed, the video is viewed again to look for discrepancies, errors, and omissions. Here are some suggestions for the video:

- A portion of a movie, especially a thriller like a Hitchcock film, with action that requires close attention to detail.

- A portion of a television show, especially any type of action show where a 5 to 10 minute segment can be used, for example, western, spy, detective, police, or hospital.

- A cartoon.

On Your Own: Students choose topics from current events and collect information for two weeks. Each student then writes an article about his or her topic, based upon the information gathered during the two week research period. One week is allowed for writing the articles. On the due date, each student hands in a scrapbook/journal of clippings and notes and an article.

76

SUGGESTIONS FOR SETTING THE STAGE

- Bring a poster to class and give the students a short time to study it (one or two minutes), then remove the poster and instruct students to list everything that was on it. When everyone has completed a list, make a composite list on the board, then bring the poster back out to look for mistakes and omissions. Discuss the impossibility of any one person remembering *everything* on the poster, but point out that different people observed and remembered different things so that, as a class, more detailed memory was possible.

- Save enough newspapers to have a "section A" for every student in the class, or tell students to bring the front-page section of a newspaper to class with them. (Alternately, assign each student to bring in one article and you can bring some newspapers for those who forget.) Instruct each student to choose an article and underline the who, what, when, where, and why in it. Then have students describe the five Ws for the articles they have chosen. In a discussion, explain the value or the purpose of the five Ws in the field of journalism, and what happens to the quality of a report if one or more are omitted.

- In a class discussion, develop a list of current events topics that could be followed for a period of time and then reported upon. This will help students when it is time for them to work on the "On Your Own" assignment.

Name _____ Date _____

INTRODUCTORY NARRATIVE

Read the following narrative to see how John learned a valuable lesson about accurately reporting a news story.

Tell It Like It Is
by John

I used to consider myself an ace reporter for my school newspaper. I'm still a reporter, but my image as an ace has been shattered. I had the opportunity of a lifetime, and I blew it because I didn't know as much about reporting as I thought I did. My dad says the experience is a "character builder," and that it will help me be a better reporter (I intend to get Bob Woodward's job some day), and I guess I agree with him. I know for sure that my reporting methods will be different from now on.

Here's what happened. I witnessed a robbery last month at Cliff's Corner Store and I wrote a story about it for the school paper. It was an important article and it was put on the front page. I was proud of it and I felt certain that it guaranteed my reputation as an ace reporter. Then, the day after my article hit the stands (or desks in this case), disaster! My best friend, Jay, came up to me before the first hour and told me that the evening news had presented a quite different story of the robbery. To put it bluntly, there were glaring discrepancies between my story and the one told by TV reporters. Throughout that day I was constantly asked why my story differed so much from that of the news media, and I tried desperately to avoid the obvious answer: I messed up.

I made several major mistakes. First, I was in a hurry. I left the scene immediately, without taking time to ask questions and find out what really happened. I wrote the article that night and turned it in just before deadline the next day, which left no time to verify my story; I relied too much on my own ability to recall details accurately; and third, I tried to be too dramatic. I guess I overestimated my skills as a reporter. I wrote an account of what I *thought* happened, but not an accurate and properly written report of what really *did* happen. My mistakes caused me quite a bit of embarrassment, especially when people asked (jokingly, I think) if they could rely on my reports about the basketball team or my "Features about Teachers" column. I can tell you, I took a lot of ribbing for a few days, and it isn't over yet. I may never live it down. Mr. Lovelace, my journalism advisor, has received over a dozen letters and notes that I truly hope will be thrown away. They are a permanent record of something I want to forget.

To clear my name somewhat, and to set the record straight, I wrote a second news report based upon interviews and newspaper accounts, and it was published in the school paper. I'm including that article here to help lay this matter to rest.

INTRODUCTORY NARRATIVE, CONT'D

Robbery at Cliff's

A daring armed robber took money and a hostage from Cliff's Corner Store Tuesday afternoon, leaving witnesses stunned but unharmed after being momentarily held at gunpoint. A suspect was arrested without incident two hours later.

Wanda Greenwell, 39, of Scottsport, was forced to drive the escape car. When she stopped at a police roadblock near Cedarville on the westbound Interstate Highway, her captor quietly released her and surrendered at approximately 6:00 p.m.

A second hostage, taken from the store with Mrs. Greenwell, was left in the parking lot. Linda Stover, 13, of Scottsport, was abducted and taken to the waiting car. There she was pushed to the ground and told to remain motionless, which she did until the car drove away.

The suspect, Alan P. Singleton, 27, claims residence in Pittsburgh, but has police records in Detroit and Chicago. He took $295 from Cliff's, all of which was returned.

Witnesses uniformly described the experience as frightening. Gary Tobias was the employee at the cash register. "The guy looked like he meant business when he ordered everyone but me to line up against the wall. He wanted me to give him money quickly so he could split. He didn't want anyone to get in his way."

Another witness, Marilyn Jenkins, added, "He waved that gun around and it scared me. I thought he might be crazy and start shooting."

This reporter can also add an eyewitness account. Seeing a loaded gun in the hand of a man wearing a ski mask is indeed frightening. The masked outlaw forced the cashier to put money in a bag and threatened to shoot anyone who moved. Then he grabbed Linda Stover by the arm and ordered Mrs. Greenwell to drive for him. The three left the store together.

It took a moment for everyone to mobilize once the danger was past. Then some people ran to help Linda Stover in the parking lot, others rushed to the shaken cashier, and someone called the police. A nervous two-hour wait ensued, until the suspect was apprehended and Mrs. Greenwell was known to be safe.

The suspect is now in the county jail awaiting arraignment on charges of armed robbery and kidnapping.

Name _____ Date _____

READING MATERIAL

The standard guidelines for journalists are the five *W*s: who, what, where, when, and why. Giving good answers to the five *W*s generally produces an informative report. But there are other rules that a journalist must follow. John neglected some of the most basic rules in his original article and, as you will see, the result was poor journalism. Here are some points to ponder before proceding with any reporting activity.

- Verify your facts: Ask questions to be sure that what you report is accurate.
- Don't guess or estimate, unless you clearly state that your report is based on guesswork.
- It is poor journalistic practice to make assumptions or draw conclusions from insufficient evidence. Don't jump to conclusions.
- Be very careful about injecting your opinions into a report. It is better to stick to the facts.
- Remain detached from the story. It may be impossible to be an unbiased reporter if you are personally involved in the event being reported.
- Report the facts as they are and let the reader draw his or her own conclusions about right or wrong, good or bad, proper or improper, appropriate or inappropriate. Don't make judgments.
- Let the truth speak for itself without trying to enhance it. Don't exaggerate.

When writing an article for a newspaper, remember these standard rules:

- Paragraphs should be short, consisting of two or three concise sentences; this makes narrow columns easier to read and allows for quick editing.
- The most important information is given first.
- More extensive (and less important) information is reserved for later in the article, where it can be cut if space needs to be conserved.
- A "lead" paragraph should grab the reader's attention while providing the basic details of the story.
- Names of witnesses, sources, victims, and others involved in a story should be given whenever possible.
- Quotes are acceptable, and even desirable, when they add interest or information to a story. The source of a quote must be identified.
- It is important to go beyond factual reporting by developing a writing style that attracts readers and holds their attention.

Read John's original article that follows, and see how many journalistic mistakes he made. You may compare it to his second effort, provided in the Introductory Narrative of this activity, to find factual errors. The second draft is correct in every way.

Cliff's Terrorized by Desperados
by John Longstreet

The world is a jungle, and there are predators out there. On February 8, at about 2:30 in the afternoon, the people at Cliff's Corner Store learned what it is to be prey in an urban jungle. This reporter was present when two deranged, bloodthirsty, armed robbers attacked the innocent people in the store and stole a large amount of money from the cash register. The first criminal, a woman, went toward the back of the store, probably to hold her gun on the victims of her vicious crime. The second, a man, waved his gun about wildly and ordered everyone in the store to line up against a wall. Both thieves wore ski masks, and their evil intent could be seen in the glint in their eyes.

When everyone was against the wall (including this reporter, who was afraid for his life after hearing threatening remarks from the man with the gun), the cashier was ordered to put money from the cash register into a paper bag. There was *lots* of money and it must have amounted to several thousand dollars. Then the man called gruffly to his companion, telling her that she would drive the getaway car, and the two of them put the finishing touch on their heinous deed by taking a young woman hostage. Forcing her to the parking lot, they knocked her out and stole her car, leaving her unconscious on the pavement. They made a clean getaway.

Inside the store, everyone was stunned. Soon, the cashier called the police and everyone else streamed into the parking lot. There lay the woman hostage, but since no gun shot had been heard it was obvious that she had just been knocked unconscious by the handle of the man's gun. The robbers were gone, probably never to be captured. It seems certain that they drove the stolen car a few blocks to their own car, took off the ski masks, changed their clothes, and melted back into the city. It seems unfair that they could get away with it, but that is exactly what happened.

This reporter has recorded this very current news event to keep the readers of our school newspaper well-informed. It is hoped that you will send your comments about such on-the-spot reporting to Mr. Lovelace in the journalism room. We will continue to provide first-hand accounts of local issues and events whenever the opportunity arises.

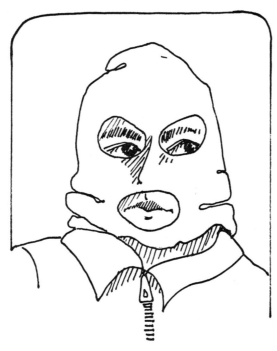

Name _____ Date _____

CLASSROOM ASSIGNMENT

You have just witnessed an event that was planned and presented by your teacher. Now your assignment is to record, as accurately as possible, what you saw and heard. In the space below, list the sequence of action as you remember it. Include as many details as possible.

When your eye witness account is finished, you will be placed in a small group to compare versions of the event. Then your group will compose a final version to present to the class.

An Eyewitness Account of an Event I Call "_____"

_____

_____

_____

_____

_____

_____

_____

_____

_____

_____

_____

_____

Name ———————————————————— Date ————————————————

ON YOUR OWN

You will become a reporter of a local, state, national, or international story by following it in newspapers, magazines, and television news reports and then writing an article summing up the information you have collected. Follow this assignment outline:

1. Choose a topic or subject area, for example:

   - The President of The United States
   - The Soviet Union
   - Arms reductions or the arms race
   - The economy
   - Natural disasters and manmade accidents
   - You may choose a local or more specific topic if something is currently happening that you would like to follow.

2. Record your topic here: ——————————————————————————

   ——

3. From today, you have two weeks to collect daily information about your topic. Keep a scrapbook or journal with all of your clippings and notes.

4. Following this two week period, you will have one week to write an article about the topic. The article should contain important details from your research without being overly long. Don't try to write about *everything,* because that would be impossible. Your job is to inform the reader about the main things that have been happening for the past two weeks within the topic area you are studying.

5. Give your article a headline.

6. On the due date hand in your scrapbook/journal and an article about your topic.

7. The due date for this project is ——————————————————————— .

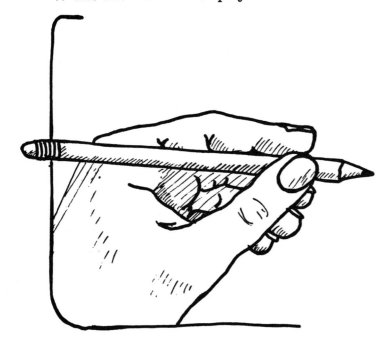

ACTIVITY 11.
Reading for Pleasure

TEACHER PREVIEW

LESSON DESCRIPTIONS

Introductory Narrative ("The Choice is Yours"): Lisa describes her successful attempt to persuade her English teacher to bring more contemporary readings into the literature class curriculum. She also introduces the "Young Adults' Choices" project, sponsored by the International Reading Association.

Reading Material: A point-by-point definition of an annotated bibliography, followed by bibliographic information about the thirty books listed in the 1988 "Young Adults' Choices," as published in the *Journal of Reading*, November, 1988.

Classroom Assignment: PREPARATION REQUIRED This lesson requires that each student have a copy of "Young Adults' Choices," either current or the one provided. "Young Adults' Choices" is published annually in a fall issue (usually October or November) of *Journal of Reading*. It is not necessary to obtain permission from the publisher to make photocopies for noncommercial educational purposes. For further information, write to:

International Reading Association
800 Barksdale Road
P.O. Box 8139
Newark, Delaware 19714-8139

Students study the annotated bibliographies provided with the "Young Adults' Choices" and choose three titles that they would like to read. For each title chosen they write a one paragraph explanation of why that book was appealing. In class, students discuss their choices and their reasons for selecting them.

On Your Own: Students choose books to read (one book per student, with teacher approval) then each prepares an entry for an annotated bibliography that is being developed by the class. The bottom portion of the Classroom Assignment Sheet is a Bibliography Form which can be filed alphabetically by title or author. It is suggested that bibliography entries be handed in in duplicate (original and copy) and filed by title *and* author. After a period of years this can become a quite extensive bibliography. The annotation should include one or more of these points:

- General story description
- Personal opinion
- Criticism
- Recommendation
- Comparison with other books or authors

SUGGESTIONS FOR SETTING THE STAGE

- Ask students to write down the name of the last unassigned book they read and briefly describe what it was about. Conduct a discussion based on their responses. Talk about the kinds of books people read and their reasons for reading. Emphasize the enjoyment one can get from reading books of personal interest. Express your sympathies to those who don't remember their last book and then discuss the value of reading on a regular basis.

- In a class discussion, develop a list of books that students would recommend to others. Ask each student to contribute at least one title to the list. Talk about what these books have that make them good enough to recommend to someone else.

Name _____ Date _____

INTRODUCTORY NARRATIVE

Read the following narrative to learn why Lisa asked her English teacher to let her read recently published novels in addition to the classic literature that her class was assigned to study.

The Choice Is Yours
by Lisa

I've never been very bold about expressing my opinions to teachers in school. I'm the type of person who accepts assignments without complaining. But there is a limit to everything, and last month when my English teacher assigned yet another reading from an author who died over a hundred years ago, I rebelled. Well, actually I asked for a private meeting with Mrs. Fitzhugh to voice my complaint. I simply had to tell her that I was dying to read contemporary books about people my own age living in my own time facing the same world I'm facing, written by authors who are still alive. Having that meeting was difficult for me, but I'm sure glad I went through with it.

I told Mrs. F. that I recognize the importance of reading classic authors like Homer, Shakespeare, Dickens, Twain, Crane, Poe, Longfellow, and all the rest. But, I asked (rather bluntly), had she considered our need to be exposed to more current material? I reminded her that the course title was "Literature"; not "Ancient" or "Classical" Literature but just "Literature." My argument boiled down to this: there must be good works of literature, recently written, that would be worth our while to study, either as a class or independently. My question to her: can we find such books and include them in the curriculum?

Mrs. F. gave my self-confidence a giant boost when she told me that I had a valid point and that she would revise the course to include some contemporary authors. From her files she dug out a copy of a magazine called the *Journal of Reading* from November, 1988, and showed me the article, "Young Adults' Choices: 1988." This was a list of thirty titles, all recently published, which were selected for their excellence by students in grades 7–12 from across the nation. The Young Adults' Choices project is sponsored by the International Reading Association, and 1987 was the first year the results of the project were published. The intent was to publish a new list of thirty titles every year, thereby providing a constant, reliable resource for finding good, current reading material. Mrs. F. told me to check this year's Young Adults' Choices. I did that, and I also studied the 1988 list carefully. I found some very interesting books, several of which I've already read.

Of course, I realize that you don't need an assignment from a teacher to read good books. But I didn't even know how to *find* good books; Young Adults' Choices helped in that respect. More important, I wanted to *study* current literature. Mrs. Fitzhugh realized that other kids did too, so she brought some new, more contemporary, books into her course.

I'm proud to take a little credit for that change. I'm also happy to have more choice in what I read, because I'm a great believer in the old adage, "variety is the spice of life."

Name ————————————————— Date —————————————————

READING MATERIAL

"Young Adults' Choices" is an annotated bibliography of the top thirty book titles for students in grades 7–12, published annually in a fall issue of the *Journal of Reading*. The titles in each year's list are selected by middle, junior, and senior high school students from across the country, the purpose being to keep young adults informed about some of the best contemporary literature being produced. By studying such a bibliography, you can learn a lot about the books, which is helpful when deciding what to read.

It is important to understand what an annotated bibliography is before trying to make use of one. Here is a list of what is included in a standard annotated bibliography.

- **Title:** Unlike some bibliographies, the one provided in the *Journal of Reading* is arranged alphabetically by title. Other bibliographies are often arranged alphabetically by the author's last name. The title is a key piece of information because it often describes the story in just a few words. Also, obviously, it makes it possible for you to find the book in a library, book store, or catalog.

- **Author's Name:** The author's name helps you associate a particular book with other works by the same person, and it also gives credit to the creator of the work. Of course, it, too, is important in locating the book.

- **Paper Edition:** If the book is available in paperback, the bibliography will tell you so with the notation, "paper ed." This will help you decide if you want to buy the book, since paperback editions are less expensive than hardcover. The letter *F* means that the paperback edition is not currently available but is forthcoming.

- **Publisher:** A complete bibliography always includes the publisher of each source cited. This gives credit for publishing the work and provides necessary information for ordering a particular book.

- **Pp.:** The number of pages is given as a notation, like "250pp." This may help you decide one way or the other about choosing a book, depending upon the amount of reading you wish to do.

- **ISBN:** The International Standard Book Number is included because it is used throughout the publishing industry as a convenient way of keeping track of the millions of books that are published. Computers know books by their ISBN rather than by their title. A typical ISBN is 0-87628-507-8.

- **Price:** The price (subject to change) is often given in U.S. dollars for both hardcover and paperback (if available). This will help you decide if you want to own the book or borrow it from the library.

- **Annotation:** "Annotated" means that each entry in the bibliography includes a description, explanation, criticism, or synopsis of the book. By reading the annotation you get an idea of what the book is about or what kind of story it tells.

The thirty titles listed alphabetically on the following pages are the "Young Adults' Choices" from the November 1988 *Journal of Reading*. Look this list over carefully to see how a bibliography is arranged *and* to discover new reading material.

Young Adults' Choices, 1988

After the Dancing Days. Margaret I. Rostkowski. Harper & Row. 224 pp. ISBN 0-06-025078-X. Paper ed., Harper Trophy. ISBN 0-06-440248-7.

Thirteen year old Annie faces the horror of war when her father, a doctor, returns from the battlefields of France in 1919 to work in a veterans' hospital. There Annie meets Andrew, a young soldier who has been severely burned. As Annie learns to see past the disfigured faces and maimed bodies, she comes to understand heroism and patriotism. One reader felt the book pictured "the tragedies of real life."

An Album of the Vietnam War. Don Lawson. Illustrated with photographs. Franklin Watts. 96 pp. ISBN 0-531-10139-8.

This illustrated history traces the war from the declaration of independence by Ho Chi Minh in 1945 to the withdrawal of U.S. troops in 1973. It describes the role of the U.S., the nature of the war itself, and the American public's increasing opposition to U.S. involvement. Concluding with a look at postwar issues, the book was "fact-filled and easy to understand," according to one reader.

Anastasia Has the Answers. Lois Lowry. Houghton Mifflin. 128 pp. ISBN 0-395-41795-3. Paper ed., Dell. F

Thirteen year old Anastasia tries to satisfy the requirements of gym class as well as to be a matchmaker for the single adults in her life. Younger teens will relate to the struggles involved in the emotional unheaval of divorce and the crushing blow to Anastasia's ego when her potential "blaze of glory" falls to the ground, and they find her " a likeable character."

The Blossoms Meet the Vulture Lady. Betsy Byars. Delacorte. 148 pp. ISBN 0-385-29485-9. Paper ed., Dell. ISBN 0-440-40677-3.

When Junior Blossom hears that there is a reward of $100 for anyone who traps a coyote that escaped from a local zoo, he decides to build the perfect trap—and ends up trapped in his own cage. Unable to free himself, he is carried off by Mad Mary, also known as the Vulture Lady, who lives in a cave. The Blos-soms "made me feel good inside," wrote one fan of the book.

The Boy Who Reversed Himself. William Sleator. Dutton. 180 pp. ISBN 0-525-44276-6.

Strange things were happening to Laura—someone was getting into her locker, papers were appearing inside with all the writing reversed, and whoever was responsible knew things about her that no one could possibly know. Inquisitive Laura becomes suspicious of Omar, the new boy next door, and he trusts her with his secrets. Readers found the story "mystifying" and "different," and one said "it allowed me to think."

Contact. Carl Sagan. Paper ed., Pocket Books. 434 pp. ISBN 0-671-43422-5.

This is an adventure story about the search for and discovery of an advanced civilization in outer space. Students found it "suspenseful—it gets more interesting as it goes on."

Count Me In. Christine McDonnell. Viking Penguin. 180 pp. ISBN 0-670-80417-7. Paper ed., Viking Penguin. ISBN 0-14-031856-9.

Katie feels she doesn't fit in anywhere. Her mother and stepfather are going to have a baby, and her father's career as a photographer prevents her from living with him. Eventually, her father's girlfriend helps her gain insight and maturity. Readers felt the book was "funny" and "true to life."

Dear America: Letters Home from Vietnam. Edited by Bernard Edelman, Paper ed., Pocket Books. 344 pp. ISBN 0-671-65684-8.

This book is more than a collection of letters. It is a gut wrenching view of human beings living in a world with more questions than answers. Many of these letters from over 100 men and women stationed in Vietnam tell a story more real and powerful than any piece of fiction. A postscript at the end of each letter tells what became of the writer or the family. Many of the letter writers were not much older than the teen who found the book "really got to me."

Finding David Dolores. Margaret Willey. Harper & Row. 162 pp. ISBN 0-06-026484-5.

Thirteen year old Arly, solitary and aloof, is drawn to an older boy, David Dolores, whom

Reprinted from *Journal of Reading* (Vol. 32, No. 2, Nov. 1988) by permission of the International Reading Association.

© 1990 by The Center for Applied Research in Education

she follows and admires from afar. She becomes friends with Regina, who joins her in spying on David. Regina's fascination with David's mother and her dislike of her own mother strain the friendship. "I wanted to jump into the book to tell Regina what I thought of her," wrote one reader.

Gillyflower. Ellen Howard. Atheneum. 128 pp. ISBN 0-689-31274-1.

Gilly Harper often hid in her secret place and made up stories about her imaginary princess, Juliana. In this way, she escaped mentally from the ugly secret that her father was sexually abusing her. The reader rejoices when Gilly learns that "Sometimes, painful things must be done to bring about happy endings. Sometimes, you have to take a chance."

Going for the Big One. P.J. Petersen. Delacorte. 196 pp. ISBN 0-385-29453-0. Paper ed., Dell. ISBN 0-440-93158-4.

The three Bates teenagers are left on their own when their stepmother runs out on them, leaving only $20. To avoid going to foster homes, they strike out through the Sierra mountains to find their father. They help a young drug dealer who has been shot and have other harrowing adventures. The book is "unpredictable" and "adventurous," according to young readers.

Heroes of the Challenger. Daniel Cohen and Susan Cohen. Paper ed., Archway. 115 pp. ISBN 0-671-62948-4.

This book gives one a greater insight into the personal and professional backgrounds of the individuals involved in the doomed space shuttle *Challenger.* It is a wise choice for students who want to quickly skim the lives of these individuals and to briefly review past and future of the space program. A student found it "very real and sad."

Holding Me Here. Pam Conrad. Harper & Row. 192 pp. ISBN 0-06-021339-6.

By snooping, Robin discovers that Mary, a boarder in her mother's house, has left her two children. Robin becomes obsessed with bringing Mary's family back together, not realizing that Mary is hiding from an abusive husband. In dealing with her guilt, Robin realizes her hurt and confusion over her own parents' divorce. "Funny, sad, frightening" and "very involving" were readers' descriptions of this book.

The Impact Zone. Ray Maloney. Delacorte. 256 pp. ISBN 0-385-29447-6. Paper ed., ISBN 0-440-94013-3.

Jim, age 15, dislikes his stepfather and idolizes his own father, a surfing photographer who left when Jim was only 9. Six years later he invites Jim to spend Christmas with him, but Jim's stepfather cancels the trip. Jim runs away to Hawaii and proves himself by surfing the treacherous Hawaiian pipeline. One reader "could picture the book as a movie."

I Never Asked You to Understand Me. Barthe DeClements. Viking Penguin. 144 pp. ISBN 0-670-80768-0. Paper ed., Scholastic. ISBN 0-590-40428-8.

Didi, trying to deal with her mother's illness and eventual death, is sent to an alternative school. She meets Stacy, whose father is sexually abusing her. Didi and Stacy work at trying to feel good again and finding solutions to their problems. Students felt the story was "about average teens" and "you could put yourself in the characters' place."

"I Touch the Future . . .". Robert T. Hohler. Random House. 276 pp. ISBN 0-394-55721-2. Paper ed., Berkley. F

The author, a journalist from Christa McAuliffe's hometown newspaper, interviewed her almost daily during her 7 months of astronaut training. The main focus is on events following Christa's application to NASA. The book details how one ordinary woman, a teacher, met the challenges of an extraordinary mission. "Christa and the other 6 astronauts will always be a part of my life," wrote one reader.

I Wear the Morning Star. Jamake Highwater. Harper & Row/Charlotte Zolotow. 160 pp. ISBN 0-06-022356-1.

This book describes Native Americans trying to combine their culture with that of 20th century America. Boarding school, foster families, and an Anglo stepfather show Sitko how far he has come from the comforting arms and beliefs of his grandma Amana, the last woman warrior of the Northern Plains Indians. This is the third book in the Ghost Horse trilogy.

Jason's Women. Jean Okimoto. Joy Street Books/Little, Brown. 224 pp. ISBN 0-87113-061-0. Paper ed., Dell. F

Jason, a self professed wimp, is a teenage boy who has difficulty approaching girls. When he places personal ads in the newspaper, it leads to two disastrous dates and a job as campaign manager for 81 year old Bertha Jane Fillmore, candidate for mayor of Seattle. The story is one that "a lot of guys can relate to" and "Jason is a hilarious character."

Middle School Blues. Lou Kassem. Houghton Mifflin. 192 pp. ISBN 0-395-39499-6. Paper ed., Avon. F

Growing up means middle school—and when Cynthia Jane Cunningham discovers that the library doesn't have a book on the subject, she decides to write her own and formulates 10 rules for survival. Kassem has captured all the anxieties, confusion, and joys of entering 7th grade. Readers of that age "could identify with some of the characters and problems."

Midnight Hour Encores. Bruce Brooks, Harper & Row. 274 pp. ISBN 0-06-020710-8. Paper ed., Harper Keypoint. ISBN 0-694-05624-3.

Sibilance T. Spooner, a 16 year old musical prodigy, suddenly decides she wants to see the mother she's never met. Her father wants Sib to understand the spirit that captured her parents in the late 1960s. Taking her across the country in an old VW bus, he talks, sings, and visits some old friends. Eventually Sib must decide whether to stay with her father or join her now wealthy mother. The story "shows how people can forgive each other," said one student.

Napoleon. Manfred Weidhorn. Atheneum. 228 pp. ISBN 0-689-31163-X.

Napoleon's life had so many strange turns it sounds like fiction. This biography describes his childhood, battlefield heroics, government problems, the exiles on Elba and St. Helena, Waterloo, and his last lonely years. Illustrations are reproductions of art from the period. "His life was an adventure," wrote one middle school reader.

Night Kites. M.E. Kerr. Harper & Row/Charlotte Zolotow. 226 pp. ISBN 0-06-023254-4. Paper ed., Harper Keypoint. ISBN 0-694-05616-2.

Although Erick Rudd's older brother always seemed perfect to him, part of Pete's life was always mysterious. Erick falls in love with a girl who is a real maverick, and their relationship falls apart when the truth about Pete is revealed. This story about a family coping with AIDS is "different from any other book."

The Other Side of Dark. Joan Lowery Nixon. Delacorte. 192 pp. ISBN 0-385-29481-6. Paper ed., Dell. ISBN 0-440-96638-8.

Seventeen year old Stacy wakes up in the hospital and discovers that she has been in a coma for 4 years. She struggles to adjust to her status as a celebrity, her own physical transformation, and the knowledge that her mother was killed by the same stranger who shot her. Stacy remembers that she saw the killer, but can't recall his identity. Several students commented "It kept you in suspense."

Pictures of Adam. Myron Levoy. Harper & Row/Charlotte Zolotow. 224 pp. ISBN 0-06-023829-1.

Lisa tells the story of her friendship with Adam, who comes from a mountain cabin and believes he is an alien from another planet. In trying to understand him, she comes to know his family and his problems. The book is touching and real in its depiction of adolescent agonies. One reader said "it was truthful—it wasn't a fake never-never-land story."

Putting on an Act. Christi Killien. Houghton Mifflin. 180 pp. ISBN 0-395-41027-4. Paper ed., Dell. F

Skeeter, a 10th grader, fantasizes about a relationship with a high school sports star and pours out the details in letters to her pen pal, Terry. Suddenly, she learns that Terry is moving to her town and she must keep her from discovering that the affair is only fantasy. The novel mirrors the plot of *A Midsummer Night's Dream,* with mistaken identity and romance for all.

A Season for Unicorns. Sonia Levitin. Atheneum. 204 pp. ISBN 0-689-31113-3. Paper ed., Fawcett. F

Conquering fears is the underlying theme of this novel. Inky fears heights and going up in a hot-air balloon. She also fears her parents will divorce. She runs away and meets a family with more love and honesty than her own. This book deals with separating reality from fantasy—that's where the unicorns come in. "It makes you feel like you've known the family forever," one reader believed.

Smart Choices. Nancy J. Kolodny, Robert C. Kolodny, and Thomas E. Bratter. Little, Brown. 368 pp. ISBN 0-316-50163-8.

In a no-nonsense tone, these essays provide advice for adolescents on handling parents, siblings, school problems, drugs, sex, and alcohol. The advice is often a series of steps or questions to answer. The book's philosophy is understanding of the temptations surrounding adolescents. This is a good reference book for students in a crisis. "It helped me with some things at home," said one high school reader.

The Solitary. Lynn Hall. Scribner's. 128 pp. ISBN 0-684-18724-8.

Jane Cahill has lived an unpleasant life with her aunt and uncle since her mother killed her father when she was 5. She realizes her dream of returning to the two room shack that belonged to her family and raising rabbits as her father had done. Her story is one of determination, hard work, and eventual success, and she finally comes to know her mother who is still in prison.

This Place Has No Atmosphere. Paula Danziger. Delacorte. 168 pp. ISBN 0-385-20489-1. Paper ed., Dell. ISBN 0-440-98726-1.

This humorous novel deals with the hurts and adjustments of moving to a new environment. In this case, the year is 2057 and 15 year old Aurora is moving to the moon! A reader found the story "hilarious—if life is going to be like that then I'll be there!"

Uneasy Money. Robin F. Brancato. Alfred A. Knopf. 246 pp. ISBN 0-394-96954-5. Paper ed., Alfred A. Knopf. ISBN 0-394-82055-X.

Who wouldn't like to win $2.5 million? This book describes the euphoria shared by 18 year old Mike and his family when he wins the state lottery, and also the troubles that instant wealth can cause. Young adults learn with Mike that happiness, loyalty, and motivation for success cannot be bought. "It seemed a lot like real life," commented one reader.

Reprinted from *Journal of Reading* (Vol. 32, No. 2, Nov. 1988) by permission of the International Reading Association.

Name _____ **Date** _____

CLASSROOM ASSIGNMENT

You have been given a copy of the "Young Adults' Choices" annotated bibliography. Take some time to read it over carefully.

If you were assigned to choose any three titles from the bibliography to read, which ones would they be? In the spaces below, write one paragraph for each of the three titles, explaining what prompted you to choose it. Why does it seem like a book you would enjoy reading? What criteria do you use for choosing your reading material? In other words, what things do you consider when selecting a book? Be prepared to discuss your choices in class.

Title 1: _____

Title 2: _____

Title 3: _____

Name _____   Date _____

ON YOUR OWN

Prepare an entry for the annotated bibliography being developed by your class. Read a book and record bibliographic information and an annotation on the form below. The top portion of this lesson will be cut off, and the Bibliography Form will be filed in duplicate, alphabetically by title and by the author's last name.

The book you choose to read must be approved by your teacher. Check with your library or your local bookstore for suggestions of good books to read.

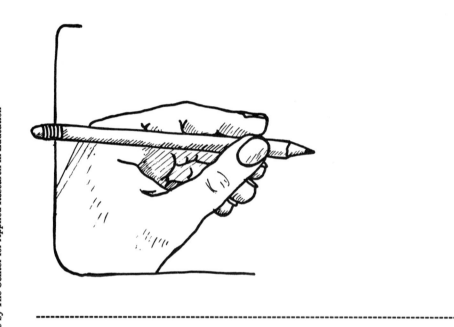

- -

Bibliography Form

_____   _____
            Title   Author (last name first)

Bibliographic Information:

Annotation.

This Bibliography Form prepared by: _____

ACTIVITY 12.
Writing for Pleasure

TEACHER PREVIEW

LESSON DESCRIPTIONS

Introductory Narrative ("A Ticket to Write"): José tells about a class he is taking called "Pleasure Writing." He explains that writing short stories is fun, and then he describes two assignments that he and his classmates were given.

Reading Material: José's paper, "Why I Like to Write Short Stories." This paper can serve as a model for students to refer to as they work on the Classroom Assignment.

Classroom Assignment: Students record types of writing that were not mentioned in the Introductory Narrative (there were ten mentioned), and in a class discussion they make a master list. Some suggestions include: biographies, autobiographies, family histories, diaries, personal letters, love letters, riddles, jokes, posters, novels, and directions or instructions. The discussion centers on whether each type of writing might be enjoyed by certain people: is it something one would do for pleasure, recreation, or personal satisfaction? After the discussion, each student writes a short paper about his or her favorite type of writing, similar to the one supplied in the Reading Material. This assignment may require two class periods to complete, especially if much time is spent discussing why people enjoy certain types of writing. Alternatively, the written portion of the assignment can be started in class and finished as homework, to be handed in the next class period.

On Your Own: Each student chooses a specific type of writing and produces a sample to be handed in. Teacher approval must be granted before students may proceed with writing. To receive approval, the assignment sheet is completed and handed in. It calls for the type of writing, the title of the project, and an outline or description of the material that will be produced. Due dates must be set for the assignment sheet and for the finished product.

SUGGESTIONS FOR SETTING THE STAGE

- Choose a very simple type of writing, such as a limerick or a haiku, and have students write about the same topic. For example, give them the first line of a limerick: "There once was a man with no car," and have them complete it, then read their versions to the class. Or, put a poster of a natural setting or situation, such as a volcano erupting or a flower beside a stream or a lion stalking a zebra, and have students describe something about it with a haiku. These, too, can be read. Talk with the class about writing for enjoyment, and point out how humorous, witty, thought-provoking, sad, or interesting each limerick or haiku is. Point out that in just a few minutes people can have fun putting ideas into words.

- Have a "micro-story" writing session. Micro-stories are very short short stories, written in a short time, like ten minutes. Give students the first sentence and then let them write until time is up. Having students read their micro-stories to the class illustrates the diversity of ideas that a single sentence can initiate. Here are some sample sentences:

  - Jennifer angrily pulled a curtain to block the shaft of light that had intruded into her room.
  - Ben laughed out loud when he realized how near he had come to misfortune.
  - A shadow ominously slid over the old brick wall.
  - The faraway sound of thunder made Sara glance apprehensively over her shoulder.
  - The old wagon tipped precariously as it careened down the hill.

- Put students in small groups (three students per group) and instruct each group to invent a product and write an outline or a script for a television advertisement. Each advertisement should answer these questions:

  - What does the product do, or what is it used for?
  - Why would a person want or need to buy the product?
  - Why should someone buy the product right now?
  - In what ways is the product superior to other, similar products?
  - Where can the product be purchased and how much does it cost?

When they are finished writing, have the groups present their advertisements. The purpose of this activity is to show how writing can be fun, so emphasize creativity and imaginative thinking.

Name _____   Date _____

INTRODUCTORY NARRATIVE

Read the following narrative to discover how José developed an interest in writing short stories.

A Ticket to Write
by José

   This year my school offered a second-semester course called "Pleasure Writing" that could be taken for credit if you got at least a "C" in first-semester English. I enrolled in it because I was told that it would be easier than second-semester English with Mr. Allen. Since I've done some writing on my own at home, I figured the course would be a breeze. It came as quite a surprise, however, to find that writing for fun isn't all that easy. I discovered that it takes concentrated effort and discipline to produce something worthwhile. I'll never forget the sense of accomplishment I felt the first time I really worked with a story; it was hard, and I struggled with it for some time before I finally found just the right words. Then I leaned back in my chair, read over what I'd written and thought to myself, "This is really good!"

   It's ironic that I've spent so much time on a class that I took to avoid work. For one of my early assignments, I chose to write a short story and I worked on it day and night for a week. I wanted it to be a good story, and I rewrote it twice before handing it in. Understand, I almost *never* redo an assignment unless I think it won't get a passing grade. In most cases, doing something once is enough. This was different, though, because my story was a personal thing; I wanted to do my best and grades had little to do with it. I would have rewritten it a third time to add some new ideas, but the due date came and I had to turn it in. I secretly hoped that my teacher would like the story and ask me to write more in the future.

   Now I am working on an assignment that asks me to explain why I like to write short stories. In class we made a list of everyone's favorite type of writing, and we talked about some of the ideas that were presented. A few, like "making lists" and "designing personal greeting cards" seemed odd at first, but the people who mentioned them gave good reasons for their choices. I can see that even making lists is an important form of writing, since it is an exercise in planning and one that I could benefit from. This assignment is helping me understand the wide range of writing interests different people have. It is also allowing me to make a statement about why I like to write short stories.

Name _____   Date _____

READING MATERIAL

Jose's writing assignment began with a discussion of types of writing that people do for pleasure, recreation, or personal satisfaction. Students in the class came up with quite a variety of suggestions, including: journals, poetry, songs, short stories, greeting cards, cartoons and comics, lists, essays, plays, and speeches. Each student had a favorite, with good reasons for preferring that particular type of writing. The discussion proved that there are many ways to enjoy writing.

Writing allows you to state opinions, vent frustrations, express emotions, tell stories, defend beliefs, organize ideas, and be creative. It can have special purpose and value to someone who writes for personal reasons. Below is José's paper. Read it carefully to get an idea of his reasons for wanting to write. Be prepared to discuss the points José makes and your own opinion about writing for pleasure—what kinds of writing do *you* like?

Why I Like to Write Short Stories
by José Berrios

From my earliest childhood I have enjoyed stories. I like to read them, hear them, and tell them. My family has a tradition of storytelling that goes back several generations. Throughout my life I have heard stories: old stories that were told by great-great-grandparents years ago, and new stories that were made up only moments before they were presented to me. The urge to tell tales was apparently inherited, and it has led me to begin writing short stories. Recording stories in permanent form offers a sense of satisfaction and enjoyment, and that means a lot to me.

One of the pleasures I get from writing is recording some of the better stories I've heard from my parents, aunts, uncles, and grandparents. Now these stories can be a part of the family forever, and anyone who wants to can read them. My grandmother was very pleased on her birthday when I gave her a written version of one of her favorite tales, which she heard from *her* grandmother years ago. It's about a little girl who earns the right to climb a mountain to gather light from the stars in order to save the life of her brother. Preserving such stories is a rewarding activity for me, but it's not the only reason I like to write.

Writing short stories is a way for me to show how I feel about things. I can create characters who think and act like me or people I admire. Or, they can behave ideally, like I think people *would* act if it were a perfect world. I can also develop characters who illustrate the opposite traits. Stories can be used to describe places I've seen, people I've known, and situations I've experienced, and to comment on issues about which I feel strongly. And, of course, writing stories provides an opportunity to complain about things that bother me and to offer possible solutions to problems that are perplexing other people.

When I write fiction I feel free to be creative. I can say anything I want in whatever style I choose. Having an outlet for creativity is important. It helps me cope with the ups, downs, joys, trials, and tribulations of life, by letting me write about them; you could say it's therapeutic. At the same time, I'm getting better and better at writing short stories, and I like the feeling of being *good* at something. It pleases me to receive compliments on a story I've written and to hear someone say "You use words so creatively; how did you learn to invent such interesting

READING MATERIAL, CONT'D

stories?" Producing a creative story is rewarding, but getting recognition makes it all the better.

There is no end to the kinds of stories that can be written. For example, my last three stories were about a boy who runs away from home and lives in an abandoned housing project, a frantic search through stellar space to find a vaccine to stop a worldwide epidemic introduced by aliens, and a young genius who discovers a way to make the world forget how to build atomic bombs. That's quite a variety, and it shows that the imagination is the only limiting factor when it comes to ideas for short stories. You can literally write a story about *anything*.

The most important point, as I've already mentioned, is that I *like* to tell stories and put them into written form. The stories don't have to carry a heavy message or a deep personal feeling. They can just be fun, enjoyable to write and enjoyable to read. Many of my stories are no more than three pages long, and they run from very serious to ridiculous and silly. I write according to my mood and immediate interest, and I'm led by my imagination, wherever it might go. A lot of energy and enthusiasm can be generated when pursuing a special interest, making a difficult task seem easy. It is hard to write a short story, but if I'm having a good time, it doesn't matter. What matters is finishing the story to my satisfaction so that I will be ready when the next inspiration comes along. That must be the definition of a true writer. If so, I guess I fit the description.

Name _____ Date _____

CLASSROOM ASSIGNMENT

This assignment has two parts, both of which are leading up to the next lesson. First you will discuss in class all the possible forms of writing that people do for fun or relaxation. Then you will write a paper about your favorite type of writing. Follow the outline below to complete the assignment:

- In a class discussion, make a list of every type of writing you can imagine, and tell if you think there are people who would do such writing for enjoyment. As a starting point, use the types of writing that José's class thought of (listed below) and then think of five more by yourself. List the five types of writing on the spaces provided. When called upon, add one of your ideas to the class list, and explain why someone might enjoy it.

Types of Writing

Journals	Songs
Poetry	Short stories
Greeting cards	Cartoons and comics
Lists	Essays
Plays	Speeches

_____

_____

_____

_____

- Now choose your favorite type of writing and compose an explanation of why you like it. Use José's paper, "Why I Like to Write Short Stories" as an example. If you never write for pleasure, then tell which type you would choose if you had to select just one for a hobby, and explain why you would prefer it over the others. Record the title below before beginning to write your paper.

Title: _____

_____

Name _____ Date _____

ON YOUR OWN

For this assignment, choose a specific type of writing that is personally enjoyable (or that you *might* enjoy if you tried it), and produce an example of that type of writing. In other words, if you enjoy poetry then you will write a poem, and if you like journals then you will write a journal entry.

Fill in the necessary information below and turn this assignment sheet in on the due date. When you receive it back with teacher approval, you may begin writing. A due date for the final product should also be recorded.

- Type of writing: _____

- Title (tentative): _____

  _____

- In the space below (and on separate paper if more room is needed) outline or describe the piece of writing you intend to produce. What topics will you cover? What message will you try to convey? How will it be organized?

- Assignment sheet due date: _____

- Final paper due date: _____

- Teacher approval of the assignment sheet

  _____ Approved: you may begin your paper.

  _____ Not approved: read my comments and see me.
  Comments:

© 1990 by The Center for Applied Research in Education

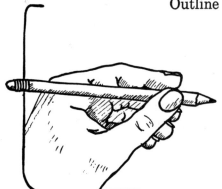

Outline or Description of the Writing Project

ACTIVITY 13.
Getting to the Point

TEACHER PREVIEW

LESSON DESCRIPTIONS

Introductory Narrative ("Don't Beat Around the Bush"): Rick explains why he admires people who are frank and straightforward when they tell you something. Then he describes a situation when he failed to live up to his ideals with one of his friends.

Reading Material: In a letter to his friend Steven, Rick tries to tell him that his (Steven's) recently completed science project is in need of more work. He does this so gently and indirectly that the message isn't clear and Steven doesn't even get the point of the letter.

Classroom Assignment: Students outline the points they think Rick really wanted to make to Steven on the assignment sheets. Then each student rewrites Rick's letter, making it more to the point. These letters may be read to the class and should be collected and graded.

On Your Own: Each student chooses one of five situations described on the assignment sheet and writes a letter to the person described. This person is assumed to be the student's good friend. Each situation shows a person with a problem, and the task of the student is to tell this friend how he or she feels about the situation and what should be done about it. Students are also given the option of developing their own situations with teacher approval.

SUGGESTIONS FOR SETTING THE STAGE

- Describe a situation, and then have a discussion about how various students might deal with it. For example, you might tell the class:

      A friend has learned how to hack his/her way into the
   school's central computer system, providing access to grade
   records and personal files. With this knowledge a person could
   change or rearrange information about anyone in the school.
   When you find out about it, your friend demands that you keep
   quiet because he/she could get into a lot of trouble. ''If you

keep it a secret,'' you are told, ''I can guarantee a 3.9 grade point average, a 1,400 total S.A.T. score, and entry into the college of your choice.'' What do you do?

- Have a class discussion in which students talk about the kinds of things they wish other people (adults or students their own age) would tell them, discuss with them, explain to them, or point out to them frankly and in a straightforward manner. Answers will range from telling someone they have spinach stuck between their teeth to explaining what AIDS is and how it is transmitted. Try to draw responses for various groups: siblings, parents, teachers, close friends, boyfriends/girlfriends, adults, and employers, for example.

- Have a discussion about the value or importance of being honest, straightforward, forthright, and frank. Do the students appreciate people who are this way with them? Is it possible to carry frankness too far? Ask students if they can think of situations where it would be best to be less than totally frank and straightforward. When is bluntness (or even truthfulness) not appropriate?

Name _____ Date _____

INTRODUCTORY NARRATIVE

Read the following narrative to see how Rick's recent attempt to be straightforward with a friend proved to be more difficult than he thought.

Don't Beat Around the Bush
by Rick

I've always admired people who were frank and to the point. There's something impressive about a person who can get to the heart of a matter without beating around the bush, or who can say what needs to be said without being offensive. That's the kind of person I want to be. I don't like indecisive people who can't tell you to your face what they think about something that is controversial or disagreeable or that deserves criticism. I want to know the truth! The unbiased, honest, straightforward opinion of someone you trust is worth more than gold, and I want to be such a person to my friends. The problem is figuring out how to be decisive, frank, straightforward, and honest without being bossy, blunt, rude, and unfeeling. It's not easy to be one without the other. Let me give an example.

My friend Steven is an easygoing guy who hates confrontation. He'll never tell you what he thinks about something if there is a chance you'll disagree. He'd rather keep his thoughts to himself. It's also difficult to tell him what *you* think about something because he may misinterpret what you're saying. His feelings are easily hurt because he thinks that if you disagree with him or criticize him it means you don't like him or are upset with him. An experience I recently had with Steven taught me a lot about being forthright. I learned that it is not easy to find the proper mix of sensitivity and straightforwardness, and I realized that it is the ability to *find* the right mix that I really admire in a person.

Last month Steven finished a science project that he had been working on for a long time. It had to do with chemistry, ionization and electricity, a topic about which I know very little. Steven planned to enter his project in the school's science fair, so he asked me to take a look at it and tell him what I thought about his display. I looked at it one afternoon while Steven was at basketball practice and was amazed at how little time and effort he had put into presenting his project. Frankly, his display was very poor, which was too bad since his ideas, hypothesis, data, and conclusions were well-documented. I was in a difficult situation because I knew how Steven reacts to criticism; but it was obvious that the display needed a major overhaul.

I went home and wrote a long letter which very gently pointed out the weaknesses of the project, and I gave it to Steven the next day. I guess I copped out, because the letter was so gentle that Steven failed to get the point. When I asked if he'd read it, he said "Yeah, thanks. I'm glad you liked it."

"For crying out loud, Steven, get that letter out and read it again!" I almost shouted.

He got it out and I read it over his shoulder. He was right: it almost sounded like I was praising his work, and it definitely did not sound very critical.

"Look, here's what I was trying to say," I said matter of factly. "Your display isn't ready for the public. It's terrible! Your writing is sloppy, there are misspelled words on your posters, and the letters on the headings are all different sizes. The electroplating experiment has no written explanation at all, and you didn't chart your data so that an idiot like me could understand what you've done. I was at a complete loss as to what you were trying to show. I had to read your report twice to figure out what the project was even about. I'm sorry, but the honest truth is that your display just isn't very good. It needs a *lot* of work! Okay?"

Tears came into Steven's eyes and his mouth dropped open. Then he walked silently away. It took a week to patch up our friendship, and another week to convince Steven that he could make a display worthy of the science fair. The "proper mix" at this time would have saved a lot of trouble and hard feelings.

Name _____ Date _____

READING MATERIAL

When Rick sat down to write a letter about Steven's science project display, his top priority was to go easy on Steven's feelings. He felt that Steven would misinterpret even the slightest criticism, so he watered the letter down and it ended up not being critical at all. When Steven read the letter he didn't get the message Rick intended; instead, he picked up on the positive things Rick said and ignored or didn't recognize the things Rick implied needed improvement. As a result, Steven accepted the letter as a statement of approval when in reality it was supposed to advise him to do some more work. This confusion led to a real problem between Rick and Steven, their friendship was temporarily damaged when Rick went to the other extreme and told Steven in very blunt terms that his project display was poorly done.

Read Rick's letter below to see how he managed to avoid telling Steven directly that he had done a poor job. As you read, try to think of how *you* might have written it so that it would be more to the point, without being insensitive or brutally frank.

Dear Steven,

I spent quite a bit of time looking at your science project this afternoon. You have done a tremendous amount of research, and your report seems to be very thorough. I spent a lot of time reading the report because I know next to nothing about ionization and electricity. I still don't really know that much, but I was impressed by the amount of data you collected from your experiments. You have page after page of it.

This project has great potential. You could take it even further than you have by thinking of an interesting way of labeling the stages of your experiment, and perhaps (if you really want to astound the judges) you could put the results of your experiment on a chart.

I like the way you have the experiment set up. I didn't realize it was an electroplating experiment until I read it in your report, but then it suddenly became crystal clear what you were trying to show. All of the wires and beakers and different colored liquids are very impressive looking. Will you be there to explain it all during the science fair? I am unclear about what happens during the experiment, but I'm sure that you will explain it to people who want to know.

I must admit that I had some trouble figuring out what your hypothesis is. I don't think it's on your poster, and I didn't find it until the last page of your report. But I *did* find it, and it seems to fit well on the last page. You might want to mention in the table of contents that the hypothesis is on the last page.

Your posters have more information per square inch than any poster I've every seen. They are *very* informative. A person could study them for a long time without getting it all. You have facts and experimental data recorded all over the place: a truly amazing collection of information. There were a couple of words that I'm not sure were correctly spelled, but you must know about them. The posters I looked at may be your rough drafts, so I'm not sure spelling mistakes need to be pointed out. That's not to say the posters look like rough drafts because they don't, really. It's just that, as with anything, you can improve posters with a little

READING MATERIAL, CONT'D

extra work, and a lot of times it's a good idea to make rough drafts first, just to get your ideas together. You probably already know that, anyway. I remember when Mr. Carson taught a unit on poster making. He said that headings were the most important features of a poster and that their appearance is critical. They are the key to a quality poster because they draw attention to a person's work. Remember? That's the only wisdom I have when it comes to posters.

Well, I guess that's about it. Just remember that the presentation makes all the rest of the work worthwhile. Without a good presentation nobody will recognize what you've done. So, with that in mind, go to it and knock'em dead at the science fair. Good luck.

Friends always,

Rick

Name ——————————————— **Date** ———————————————

CLASSROOM ASSIGNMENT

This assignment is based upon Rick's letter to Steven. In the space below, make an outline of the points you think Rick really wanted to make to Steven. Include everything you can think of. It may be helpful to reread Rick's narrative and letter and underline anything that might contribute to your understanding of what Rick was trying to say. Be prepared to hand your outline in if asked to do so.

Next, rewrite Rick's letter so that it makes all of the points you've outlined in a sensitive, straightforward way. Your letter will be handed in and may be read to the class. Pretend that you are Rick and address the letter to Steven. Be sure that he understands clearly what needs to be done to get ready for the science fair, but also take into account his personality and his normal reaction to criticism.

An Outline for Rick's Letter to Steven

Name _____ Date _____

ON YOUR OWN

Choose a situation from the list provided below and write a letter to the person involved. You may expand the scope of the situation or add details if you want to focus on specific points in your letter. Assume the person to whom you are writing is a close friend. Before writing, outline the main points you want to make. Be as concise and straightforward as possible, but also show understanding and compassion. In the letter you are to explain how *you* feel about the situation. Offer advice, criticism, or moral support, and give your friend suggestions or ideas. Above all establish your own point of view so that your friend knows exactly where you stand on the issue. Write the letter in a conversational tone, as if you were talking to your friend face to face.

Keep in mind that these situations deal with very difficult issues and there are no perfect solutions. This assignment is to see how you might respond if such a situation were to develop in the life of one of your friends.

- Your friend's brother is a hemophiliac and has contracted AIDS from a blood transfusion. People are opposed to his coming to school or having contact with their children in any way. How do you feel? What should be done about your friend's brother's schooling? How should your friend react? What can be done?

- Your friend has become seriously depressed over family problems, boyfriend/girlfriend difficulties, dropping grades, conflicts with teachers, and lowering self-esteem, and has mentioned suicide. What can you say? How can your friend be shown that life is worth living and that you will be there for moral support? How can you convince your friend to *talk* with someone about his or her problems?

- Your friend is becoming involved with a boyfriend/girlfriend that you strongly feel is a bad influence on him/her. You see your friend losing interest in school, running with a crowd that gets in trouble a lot, developing an "I don't care" attitude, and intentionally allowing grades to slip and old friendships to dissolve. After a fight with the boyfriend/girlfriend, your friend asks for advice. What do you say?

- Your friend has been cheating to get good grades and you just found out about it. Now you discover that he/she plans to hand in a research paper that was written three years ago by another friend's older sister. The paper is very well written and it received an *A* when it was first submitted. That is why your friend is interested in it. What would you say to this person if he/she talked to you about it?

- Your friend has begun to experiment with drugs and alcohol, and was recently involved in an alcohol-related car accident with some of his/her friends, in which two people were seriously injured. Now is an excellent time to convince your friend that drugs are dangerous. How do you do it? What do you say?

- You may develop your own situation with teacher approval. Record it here:

_____ Approved
_____ Needs improvement

Comments:

ACTIVITY 14.
Writing a Biography

TEACHER PREVIEW

LESSON DESCRIPTIONS

Introductory Narrative ("A Real-Life Story"): Angela relates how she became interested in the life and exploits of Alexander the Great when, as an elementary student, she read about his horse, Bucephalus. Then she explains that an assignment from her social studies teacher gave her an opportunity to write a short biography of Alexander.

Reading Material: Angela's biography of Alexander the Great. Students should be encouraged to analyze and discuss how it is written to help them prepare to write biographies of their own.

Classroom Assignment: Students identify people about whom biographies could be written. These people all come from a historical period or special category that you designate before the activity begins. Examples include: twentieth-century England, European monarchies, Chinese dynasties, explorers, Renaissance artists, the presidency, World War II, American writers, the Industrial Revolution, and the Great Depression. Students are asked to verify that enough information is available by finding references to these people in history books, encyclopedias, and general references. After students complete their lists, a master list is developed in a class discussion. This assignment is best conducted in a library or resource room.

On Your Own: Each student chooses one of the names from the master list developed in class and looks for three good sources of information about that person. These sources are recorded in proper bibliographic form and handed in for approval. Upon receiving approval, students write short biographies (five to eight handwritten pages) of the people they have chosen to study.

SUGGESTIONS FOR SETTING THE STAGE

- In a class discussion (with students taking notes) develop a list of things to consider when writing a biography. No item is too insignificant. Get students to think about what a person must do to prepare for such a project as well as what should be included in a well-written biography. Be prepared to add anything to the list that the students fail to think of, so that at the end of the discussion it reflects your goals for the biography project. Emphasize these goals as you make each assignment so that students can see the continuity that is necessary to take an idea from the brainstorming stage to a finished product.

- Provide students with maps of the ancient world, and have them trace the path taken by Alexander the Great as he conquered territory from the Dardanelles to beyond the Indus River. Describe a few of his exploits, or give a detailed account of one of his battles (his defeat of King Porus at the river Hydaspes would make a good story, as would a description of Hephaestion's funeral). This activity will help students understand Alexander's biography in geographical terms, which is very important.

Name _____ Date _____

INTRODUCTORY NARRATIVE

Read the following narrative to learn how Angela turned an assignment from her social studies teacher into an opportunity to read and write about one of her favorite historical characters.

A Real-Life Story
by Angela

Bucephalus. It was Bucephalus that made me realize how interesting history can be. He doesn't know about his influence on me, of course. He's dead. He's been gone for over 2,000 years now, but his legend lives on. The first time I read about Bucephalus and his times, I knew I had to learn more.

Bucephalus was a horse. A proud, powerful, highly spirited war horse. His owner was Alexander the Great, one of the most successful conquerors of all time. I had never heard of Alexander the Great until I read about Bucephalus in a book about horses. I was eleven years old at the time, and I was fascinated by horses. I read everything I could get my hands on, and I wanted a horse so badly that I cried every time my dad explained why we could never have one.

Anyway, one day at the library I found a book about horses in myth, legend, and history. Near the front was a drawing of a huge, beautiful horse being ridden bareback by a twelve year old boy, while a large group of soldiers and older men looked on in disbelief. No one else had been able to mount Bucephalus, but Alexander gained his trust immediately and was able to mount and ride him with ease. I must admit that I had an instant crush on the twelve-year-old Alexander. I decided then and there that I had to find out more about him, and I've been learning about Alexander the Great and the ancient Greeks ever since. Over the years my hobby has made me something of an expert.

Recently, an assignment from my social studies teacher, Mr. Brown, gave me an opportunity to put my knowledge of Alexander the Great to good use. He asked each student to choose a topic from ancient history (we could choose any topic, with his approval, and make a visual, written, or oral presentation on it. Some people made oral presentations, a few produced written reports, and one or two built dioramas, but most chose to produce informative posters. I was the only one in the class to write a biography. Because it was not on the list of project choices, I asked for permisson, and Mr. Brown said it was a good idea.

I worked very hard on my biography of Alexander the Great. I tried to write it so that someone my age could understand who he was, what he did, and why he is an important historical figure. In the process I learned that writing a biography is a fun way to study history. I really enjoyed the project and now I'm looking for an opportunity to write another one (perhaps about Alexander's friend and general, Ptolemy, who was the ancestor of Cleopatra, Queen of Egypt). Wouldn't it be something if some day, when people ask me what I do, I could say "I'm a writer. I write biographies." I like the sound of that.

Name _____ Date _____

READING MATERIAL

A biography is a description of a person's life, as told by someone who has access to reliable information. A good biographer must be a competent researcher because accurate facts are the most important feature of a useful biography. A good biographer must also be able to blend facts together into a form that is enjoyable to read. Read Angela's biography of Alexander the Great below and see if you think she did a good job of writing about his life. Keep in mind that there is much more she *could* have written, but she was restricted by a page limit that forced her to be selective and carefully organize her information.

The Story of Alexander the Great
by Angela Feldman

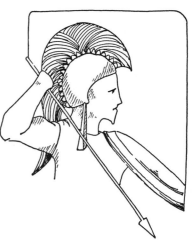

The story of Alexander the Great begins in the tiny kingdom of Macedon, in the year 356 B.C., where he was born the first son of King Philip II. It ends thirty-three years later in Babylon, by which time Alexander had conquered most of the ancient world and had been proclaimed a god.

When Alexander's father was murdered at his own wedding (after divorcing Alexander's mother, Olympias), Alexander became Alexander III, King of Macedon and ruler of most of the surrounding territories. Almost immediately, however, the city-states of central Greece, called the Corinthian League, and the barbarians of the north rebelled against the young king. Acting swiftly and confidently, Alexander snuffed out each rebellion and firmly established himself as leader of the Greek world. He then began preparations for an invasion of Asia with the army his father had organized. Philip II had planned to free Greek city-states along the shore of what is now Turkey from the control of the King of Persia, Darius III. Alexander, however, had even bigger things in mind.

What kind of a man was Alexander? He was confident, that's for sure. He was famous for riding the fearsome war horse, Bucephalus, at the age of twelve when no other man could approach the animal. He had the strong support of his army; he knew several thousand soldiers by name, an amazing feat which gave him great power of persuasion over his men. He was a runner of Olympic quality. He loved music and theater, and he could not live without his beloved *Iliad*—he slept with it under his pillow, along with his dagger, and read excerpts from it to his officers. He was a leader in the truest sense: in battle he was always first, ahead of his soldiers, leading the charge. He was also generous with the spoils of war.

Darius III seemed unconcerned about Alexander, however, and failed to prepare for him. At the river Granicus, Alexander easily won his first encounter with a Persion army unit. He then methodically marched on the cities along the Aegean and Mediterranean Seas. Soon he had control of all the ports used by the fearsome Persian navy, which left the Persian army without sea support. All this finally got Darius's attention, and he headed out from Babylon to meet Alexander with a huge army of perhaps 600,000 men.

Alexander's army, with only 30,000 infantry soldiers and 5,000 calvary riders, was obviously outnumbered, but his superior military tactics won him a decisive victory. In fact, Darius retreated so quickly that he left behind his entire family and his treasure train filled with gold, silver and jewels. Alexander now had valuable hostages and the money he needed to continue his campaign.

READING MATERIAL, CONT'D

Rather than chase Darius, Alexander headed south, taking city after city along the eastern coast of the Mediterranean sea. Most gave up without a fight, but Tyre required a seven-month seige before he took it with an attack by ships, supported by catapults set up on an arm of land he built out into the sea. The two-month seige of Gaza followed, and from there Alexander and his army marched into Egypt, where he was placed on the throne and hailed as Pharaoh. He was called Son of Ammon, a god. In Egypt, he founded the city of Alexandria, which still exists. He was King of Macedon, King of Greece, and King of Egypt, but he still had work to do, for Darius was in Babylon raising another army.

Alexander met the Persian army for the third and final time in 331 B.C. at Gaugamela. The result was another defeat for Darius, who was killed in his desperate flight by one of his own officers. Alexander was recognized as the Great King of Persia.

Still driven to conquer, Alexander crossed the Himalyas into India in 327 B.C., even though his army was not happy about it and his generals advised against it. In the middle of monsoon season he crossed a raging river in the face of the Indian King Porus's army, which included many war elephants. There he won perhaps his most remarkable victory. He pushed on to the Hyphasis River, but here his army finally refused to go further; they were tired and they wanted to go home.

For three days Alexander sulked in his tent, refusing to talk to anyone. Finally accepting that he had gone as far east as possible, he decided to take a new route home (always the explorer and adventurer!), so his army marched south along the Indus River all the way to the Arabian sea. Here he put part of his men in boats and sent the fleet home, and the rest he marched west across the deserts of what is now southern Pakistan and Iran. The march was a disaster. The fleet was supposed to supply the army from the sea, but it was caught in monsoons and couldn't move for weeks. Only a quarter of the army survived the trip, the rest being left along the train where they fell of thirst or sunstroke.

Surviving undaunted himself, Alexander headed toward Babylon, where he planned to organize his next expedition, a military campaign into Arabia. In June, 323 B.C., however, he became sick and twelve days later he died, most probably of malaria, complicated by his old war wounds, including one from an arrow that had pierced his lung.

Alexander's empire had lasted less than ten years, and now generals and armies scrambled for power. But through the turmoil, Alexander's funeral train, carrying his embalmed body, made its majestic way. The coffin was made of beaten gold, and it had taken two years to build the magnificent wagon that carried it. Month after month the most extravagant procession even seen in the western world slowly followed the road builders across Asia Minor. Stopping in every town for sacrifices, songs, and prayers, it worked its way for over a thousand miles to its final resting place in Egypt, first in Memphis, then in "The Tomb" in Alexandria: Alexander's city. One man had left his mark on history forever.

© 1990 by The Center for Applied Research in Education

Bibliography

BOWDER, DIANA, ed. *Who Was Who in the Greek World.* New York: Washington Square Press, 1982.

COTTERELL, ARTHUR, ed. *The Encyclopedia of Ancient Civilizations.* New York: Mayflower Books, Inc., 1980.

DURANT, WILL. *The Story of Civilization II: The Life of Greece.* New York: Simon and Schuster, 1966.

HOOPER, FINLEY. *Greek Realities: Life and Thought in Ancient Greece.* Detroit: Wayne State University Press, 1984.

PALMER, R.R., ed. *Historical Atlas of the World.* New York: Rand McNally & Co., 1980.

RENAULT, MARY. *The Nature of Alexander.* New York: Pantheon Books, 1976.

STARR, CHESTER G. *The Ancient Greeks.* New York: Oxford University Press, 1981.

Name _____   Date _____

CLASSROOM ASSIGNMENT

In the space below, list fifteen names of people about whom informative biographies could be written and explain what they are known for. These people should come from the historical period or special category (the Renaissance, or New World Explorers, for example) that you are studying. Use history books, text books, encyclopedias, and other general references to find these names and to verify that enough information is available to write a biography about each person. Be prepared to share your list with the class in a discussion designed to produce a master list of possible biography subjects.

Historical period/Special category: _____

_____

FIFTEEN BIOGRAPHY SUBJECTS

Name	Known for . . .
1. _____	_____
2. _____	_____
3. _____	_____
4. _____	_____
5. _____	_____
6. _____	_____
7. _____	_____
8. _____	_____
9. _____	_____
10. _____	_____
11. _____	_____
12. _____	_____
13. _____	_____
14. _____	_____
15. _____	_____

Name _____ Date _____

ON YOUR OWN

Choose one person from the list developed in class and record it on the line below, beneath the historical period or special category that you are studying. In the space provided, identify at least three sources that you find, from which enough information can be obtained to write a biography about the person you have chosen. Record these sources as a bibliography.

When your bibliography is returned with teacher approval, begin writing a biography. The biography should be five to eight handwritten pages (three to five typewritten) long, and it is due on the date recorded below. Hand in a bibliography with your finished paper, adding any new sources that you may have used.

Historical period/special category: _____

_____

Person being studied: _____

Biography due date: _____

Teacher approval: _____

More work needed (see notes on back): _____

Bibliography

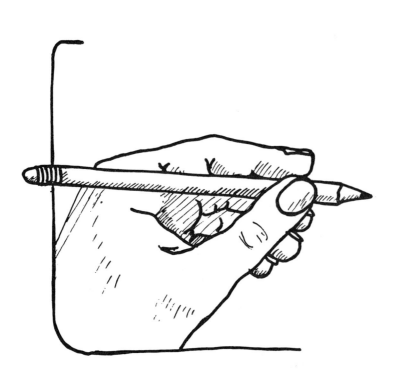

ACTIVITY 15.
Describing Characters

TEACHER PREVIEW

LESSON DESCRIPTIONS:

Introductory Narrative ("Words of a Master: Charles Dickens") Caleb describes how he became interested in reading Charles Dickens' stories after being assigned to find examples of character descriptions by famous authors.

Reading Material: Character descriptions from *Pickwick Papers* by Charles Dickens.

Classroom Assignment: Students rewrite Charles Dickens' character descriptions, using modern language to describe a fictional person who lived in England over 100 years ago. Each student works from one of the excerpts in the Reading Material; students may also search through books to find other Dickens characters to describe (with your approval). Descriptions are read in class and then handed in.

On Your Own: Students write detailed character descriptions as if they were being developed for a short story.

SUGGESTIONS FOR SETTING THE STAGE

- Come to class with character descriptions from a variety of authors and have students read them orally. Provide time between readings to discuss each author's style, use of vocabulary, and effectiveness in creating a mental image. Or, assign students to find and bring in character descriptions of their own to read.

- Bring in posters or pictures of interesting people and have students think of words or phrases that describe each character. In a class discussion ask students to explain why they chose certain words to describe the characters.

- Have students write character descriptions of themselves.

- Ask a guest to come to your class dressed in a costume of some type, and casually pose or walk about the room for twenty minutes while students write brief character descriptions. This guest could be a member of a drama club, a character in a school play, an actor from a local theater group, or it could just be someone willing to volunteer to help with your class. After twenty minutes of writing, have students read their descriptions orally.

Name _____ **Date** _____

INTRODUCTORY NARRATIVE

Read the following narrative to find out how Caleb became interested in the writings of Charles Dickens as he learned how to write character descriptions.

Words of a Master: Charles Dickens
by Caleb

During the summer, when I found out that my school's English teacher, Mrs. Smithson, had moved and a new teacher would be hired, I was shocked. My friends and I knew Mrs. Smithson and how she taught. Her classes were boring, but it was easy to get good grades from her. Now I was faced with the prospect of having to deal with a new, probably inexperienced, English teacher who undoubtedly would be both a tough grader and very strict.

On the first day of school, Mr. Johnston made his debut. I have never had a teacher quite like him. He said he was going to make *writers* of us; this would be accomplished by letting us *write*. He started out on the very first day by talking about short stories. He said every one of us had a short story inside, just waiting to be written. I've always enjoyed writing such things as notes to my friends, letters to pen pals, silly poems, and stories for my own enjoyment. The idea of learning how to write short stories appealed to me, because I thought I could be good at it.

My first assignment from Mr. Johnston was to find a character description by a famous author to bring to class for discussion. This was the first step toward learning to write character descriptions, which would help in our future attempts at writing short stories. The assignment stumped me for a while. I had not read many books by famous authors, and I didn't know where to begin looking. Finally, I decided to go to the library to ask for help. The librarian told me that some of the best character descriptions she'd ever read were written by Charles Dickens and that one of his best books, filled with descriptions of many different people, was *Pickwick Papers*. I found the book, checked it out, and took it home. I had never read anything like it. Although it was written a long time ago, the story was hilarious, and the librarian was right: it was filled with excellent character descriptions. When I took the book to school and read some excerpts, everyone agreed that Charles Dickens was very good at describing the characters in his stories.

Name ——————————————— Date ———————————————

READING MATERIAL

Character descriptions are important components of a short story or novel. Each character has a role to play or a reason for being in the story. The reader should have a mental image of what characters look like, what they sound like, how they think, and how they act. This adds interest and appeal to the story.

You can learn a great deal about describing characters by reading the works of a master writer like Charles Dickens. Dickens lived in another time; the characters he describes come out of mid-nineteenth century England. Do you think you could describe a character from the late twentieth century that would be interesting to a reader in the year 2130? Dickens has preserved characters for well over one hundred years by carefully and creatively describing them to his readers. It isn't necessary to read his massive novels in their entirety to learn from him about character development. As you read the following excerpts, take note of how well written they are and remember that you are reading the words of a master.

Excerpts from Charles Dickens' *Pickwick Papers*

1. He was about the middle height, but the thinness of his body and the length of his legs gave him the appearance of being much taller. The green coat had been a smart dress-garment in the days of swallow-tails, but had evidently in those times adorned a much shorter man than the stranger, for the soiled and faded sleeves scarcely reached to his wrists. It was buttoned closely up to his chin, at the imminent hazard of splitting the back; and an old stock, without a vestige of shirt-collar, ornamented his neck. His scanty black trousers displayed here and there those shiny patches which bespeak long service, and were strapped very tightly over a pair of patched and mended shoes as if to conceal the dirty white stockings, which were nevertheless distinctly visible. His long black hair escaped in negligent waves from beneath each side of his old pinched-up hat; and glimpses of his bare wrists might be observed between the tops of his gloves and the cuffs of his coat-sleeves. His face was thin and haggard, but an indescribable air of jaunty impudence and perfect self-possession pervaded the whole man.

2. The man had moved into a sitting posture. His body was much bent, and his face was wrinkled and yellow. His dress denoted him an inmate of the workhouse; he had the appearance of being very old, but it looked more the effect of dissipation or disease than length of years. He was staring hard at the stranger, and though his eyes were lustreless and heavy at first, they appeared to glow with an unnatural and alarmed expression after they had been fixed upon him for a short time, until they seemed to be starting from their sockets.

3. He was a prim-faced, red-nosed man, with a long, thin countenance, and a semi-rattlesnake sort of eye: rather sharp, but decidedly bad. He wore very short trousers and black cotton stockings, which, like the rest of his apparel, were particularly rusty. His looks were starched, but his white neckerchief was not, and its long limp ends straggled over his closely buttoned waistcoat in a very uncouth and unpicturesque fashion. A pair of old, worn beaver gloves, a broad-brimmed hat, and a faded green umbrella with plenty of whale-bone sticking through the bottom as if to counterbalance the want of a handle at the top, lay on a chair beside him, and being disposed in a very tidy and careful manner, seemed to imply that the red-nosed man, whoever he was, had no intention of going away in a hurry.

Charles Dickens, *Pickwick Papers* (The New American Library, Inc., 1964), pp. 32, 107, and 405.

Name _____   Date _____

CLASSROOM ASSIGNMENT

Charles Dickens was a genius when it came to descriptive writing. His contemporary audience lived in England over one hundred years ago, and he used words, phrases, and a writing style that are not common today. This assignment asks you to become a "ghost writer" for Charles Dickens by writing a description of one of his characters for a modern audience.

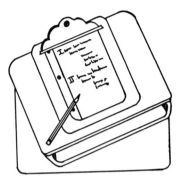

Choose a character description from a Charles Dickens story; use one of the three excerpts provided in the Reading Material, or, with teacher approval, select another character from one of Dickens' novels. Read the description several times until you get a mental image of what the person must have looked like. Then write your own description of the *same character,* but in terms that a modern American would understand. Be prepared to read your work to the class.

I have chosen:

_____ excerpt 1
_____ excerpt 2
_____ excerpt 3
_____ Another Charles Dickens' character description
Name of book: _____
Page _____ Include a copy of Dickens' description with your completed assignment.
Teacher approval: _____
Approval withheld: _____

Comments:

Name _____ Date _____

ON YOUR OWN

When you write a story you are creating visual images out of words, for the benefit of a reader. You can become good at this type of writing with practice. It is like being an artist with a dictionary: a writer paints pictures with words. One of the most critical parts of most fiction is *character development.*

Write a character description that could be used in a short story. This description should come out of your own imagination. Choose at least two categories from the list below and make them the focal points of your description.

- Personality
- Thought process (how the person *really* thinks about things)
- Stature/size/posture/shape
- Clothing
- Facial expressions
- Physical characteristics (examples: eye color, birth marks, type and color of hair)
- Habits/mannerisms
- Health/hygiene
- Type or quality of voice
- How the character fits into the setting

You may choose to write about one of the characters listed below, or you may invent your own character. This list is provided to help you begin thinking about character descriptions:

- An athlete in an important game
- A student at school dressed in the latest style, fashion, or fad
- A character from your neighborhood
- A parent in a typical situation, like getting ready for work in the morning
- A teacher in a classroom situation
- A bum in an alley
- A beauty queen
- A rock star on stage
- A boy asking a girl for a date, or vice versa
- Other: _____

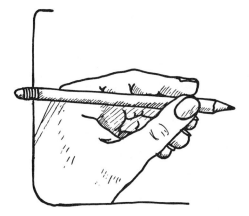

ACTIVITY 16.
Presenting Information Visually

TEACHER PREVIEW

LESSON DESCRIPTIONS

Introductory Narrative ("A Poster's Worth a Thousand Words"): Paul tells of his first attempt at presenting information about Saturn to a fifth grade audience. He then explains how he recognized the value of visual aids when his friend used a poster to help her audience follow and understand her presentation about the Moon.

Reading Material: An information sheet about posters, with a list of suggestions for making a good poster.

Classroom Assignment: Using facts about Saturn provided on the assignment sheet, students make rough drafts of posters that Paul could have used in his presentation to fifth graders.

On Your Own: Each student chooses a topic from a subject area that you assign. The subject area may be very broad (biology, for example), general (insects), or specific (butterflies). It may be from virtually any discipline and apply directly to something that is already being taught. Once topics are chosen and approved, students produce well-made, informative posters.

SUGGESTIONS FOR SETTING THE STAGE

- Discuss occupations that require individuals to make presentations, teach, or communicate information and ideas to others. List these occupations on the board as they are suggested by students. Ask how many are considering careers in any of the areas listed. Suggest that junior and senior high school are the places to learn how to make effective presentations, *as a step in preparing for a career.* Then focus the discussion on the usefulness and value of visual aids to people who make presentations. Mention posters as a specific type of visual aid that is used by many students and talk about the importance of learning how to make a good one.

- Play a game of Pictionary (played like the T.V. game show "Win, Lose, or Draw") with the class, by dividing students into small teams. Use the game as the basis for a discussion about the value of visual communication. Talk about the drawings that were used: why did some drawings get correct answers and others didn't? This discussion can lead to the use of visual aids when making presentations, which in turn can be an introduction to a discussion about posters.

120

Name _____ Date _____

INTRODUCTORY NARRATIVE

Read the following narrative to learn how Paul discovered the value of putting information into visual forms for presentation to others.

A Poster's Worth a Thousand Words
by Paul

My introduction to the value of visual aids came as I was standing before a class of fifth graders, struggling to get through a lecture I had prepared about Saturn. My astronomy club had agreed to put together some lessons about the solar system and present them to elementary classes in the district. My topic was Saturn. I was deeply into the presentation when I noticed that the attention of my audience had drifted somewhat. As I looked around the room it was obvious that most of the class had lost track of what I was talking about. When I asked them to recall what I'd said about Saturn's density, I knew my debut as a teacher was a flop. "What's density?" asked one student.

Exasperated, I explained for the third time that it's the mass of one cubic centimeter of a substance. The density of water, for example, is one gram per cubic centimeter. The density of Saturn is less than one because it is made mostly of liquid hydrogen, which is less dense than water. "Is that clear now?" I asked. The response from another student proved that I had real problems: "What did you say hydrogen is?" Realizing that no one was retaining anything I said, I grew frustrated, hurried through the rest of my presentation, and sat down. It was discouraging because I was scheduled to talk about Saturn to at least ten more classes during the year, which suddenly seemed like an unappealing idea.

Following my presentation, my fellow astronomy club member, Nancy, got up to present her topic: the Moon. She had with her a carefully made poster that was filled with pictures, charts, and facts. Drawing the students' attention to the poster, Nancy began talking to them about the Moon. She had their attention! They could *see* what she was talking about! I was very impressed by the role Nancy's poster played in her presentation, and I soon made one of my own on Saturn. It really did make a difference. Students could refresh their memories by looking at the poster while I talked, and it gave me something to refer to when I introduced a new idea. Now I understand that presenting information visually is an important part of communication, and that's a lesson I won't forget.

Name _____ Date _____

READING MATERIAL

An important part of most presentations is a visual display of information. The focus of this activity is on posters, but it should be clear that there are many other forms of visual presentation, including murals, collages, dioramas, models, exhibits, displays, demonstrations, plays, scrapbooks, reenactments, mobiles, video shows, slide shows, computer programs, and photographs. Much of what this activity teaches about posters applies equally well to these other methods of presenting information.

Read the lesson about posters and then *use* what you have learned from this activity the next time you are required to make an informative presentation.

Posters

Making posters is one of the common requirements of students working on research assignments, science fair projects, classroom presentations, or independent study activities. A poster shows what you have learned about a subject; it is a way of making your knowledge available to others, even when you're not around to talk with them. A person who has learned how to produce a well-made, informative poster has a very important skill that will be used over and over again.

Here is a list of suggestions for making a good poster. Keep these things in mind (and *practice* them), and you will be surprised at the quality of your finished product.

- Always make a rough draft of a poster before beginning the final version. A rough draft helps determine how big drawings should be and where they should be positioned; it allows experimentation with headings and captions; it provides an idea of how much space is available and how much written material can be used; and it lets you change your mind, try new ideas, and start over if you wish. Remember: "rough" means preliminary, not sloppy.

- Take time to think about the poster before beginning to work on it.

- Use light pencil guidelines for all writing. Crooked, slanted, or disorganized writing is difficult to read and gives a bad impression of your work.

- Supply a heading or title in large letters that explains what the poster is about.

- Include only accurate information: be *sure* of your facts!

- Produce at least one original drawing, chart, graph, or other art work that helps illustrate the topic.

- Do all writing and drawing *lightly* in pencil before adding color so that mistakes can be corrected.

- Make all headings the same color. Do *not* make every letter a different color.

- Every word on the poster must be spelled correctly. Misspelled words are simply not acceptable: they make it seem as if you either don't care about your work or don't know much about your topic.

- Organize the poster so that it is easy to understand. Make drawings clear and uncluttered, keep facts simple and to the point, include enough information to make the poster worth reading or studying, and place emphasis on neatness and attractiveness to ensure that people will *want* to look at it.

- Put a border around the poster. This can be as simple as leaving a margin of an inch or so around the outer edge, or as complex as matting and framing it. Sometimes a simple dark border of uniform width is all that is necessary to make a poster look nice.

- Put your name, grade, and school on the *front* of the poster: be proud of your work and let everyone know who did it.

Name _____ Date _____

CLASSROOM ASSIGNMENT

The information that Paul collected for his presentation about Saturn is provided below. Each fact is listed in the order that it was recorded on a notecard (Paul's method of collecting facts), so similar or related facts are not necessarily grouped together. Read the facts over carefully, to become familiar with them, then complete the following assignment:

1. Make a rough draft of a poster that Paul could have used with his presentation.

   a. Choose at least fifteen of the facts listed below. Write them (or illustrate them) in whatever way you wish.
   b. Sketch an illustration. Spend some time on the sketch. Don't just scribble something: be as precise and artistic as possible.
   c. Design a simple border.
   d. Give the rough draft a heading.
   e. Even though this is a rough draft, do your best work on it. Think your ideas through before beginning.

2. Hand the rough draft in. Be prepared to show it to the class and to explain your work if called upon.

Facts About Saturn

- Saturn's diameter is 74,500 miles.
- Saturn is 886,700,000 miles from the sun.
- Saturn rotates about its axis in 10 hours 40 minutes.
- It takes 29.6 Earth years for Saturn to revolve around the Sun.
- If you weighed 100 pounds on Earth, you would weigh 132 pounds on Saturn.
- Saturn has 22 moons.
- Saturn is the sixth planet from the Sun.
- If Saturn were hollow, 800 Earths could fit inside it.
- Saturn has more moons than any other planet.
- Traveling at 31,000 miles per hour, it took the Voyager spacecraft a little more than three years to reach Saturn.
- Saturn's magnetic field is a thousand times stronger than Earth's.
- Saturn is the second largest planet in the solar system (behind Jupiter).
- Galileo first looked at Saturn through a telescope in 1610. He called the rings "ears."
- Fierce storms rage in Saturn's clouds, with winds up to 1,100 miles per hour.
- Saturn's air is mostly hydrogen and helium with some ammonia and methane mixed in.
- The rings of Saturn are really more than 1,000 separate rings.
- The distance from the inner edge of the rings to the outer edge is more than 45,000 miles.
- The thickness of the rings is very thin: from only 30 feet to 500 feet.
- The rings are made of ice and dust. Particles range from the size of a grain of salt to the size of a railroad boxcar.

CLASSROOM ASSIGNMENT, CONT'D

- It seems that the rings are held together by Saturn's moons: their gravity keeps the rings "fenced in."
- The largest moon is Titan.
- All of the moons contain water, and ice; some contain rock, too.
- Titan is the only moon in the solar system with an atmosphere; it is a dense atmosphere that glows with a reddish-orange light.
- Saturn does not have a solid surface; it is a sphere of liquid gas, mostly hydrogen and helium, just like the air around it.
- The diameter of Saturn's rings is 170,000 miles.
- Saturn is the least dense planet in the solar system.
- The distance from Saturn's surface to the inner edge of the rings is about 7,000 miles.
- The two *Voyager* probes examined Saturn in 1980 and 1981.
- Saturn is the last planet visible to the naked eye.
- Saturn's density is less than 1 gram per cubic centimeter, which means it would float in water if a large enough ocean could be found.

Bibliography

GALLANT, ROY A. *The Macmillan Book of Astronomy*. New York: Macmillan, 1986.

JOHNSON, OTTO et al., eds. *The 1988 Information Please Almanac*. Boston: Houghton Mifflin, 1988.

MAYALL, NEWTON R., MARGARET MAYALL, and JEROME WYCKOFF. *The Sky Observer's Guide*. New York: Western Publishing Co., Inc., 1985.

MCALEER, NEIL. *The Cosmic Mind-Boggling Book*. New York: Warner Books, Inc., 1982.

Name _____ Date _____

ON YOUR OWN

Choose a topic from the subject area your teacher has assigned, and make an informative poster about that topic. For example, if the subject area is biology, you might choose insects for a topic; if the subject area is insects, you might choose butterflies; if the subject area is butterflies, you might choose monarch butterflies. In any of these cases, you would design and produce a poster that presents information about your topic.

Record your topic choice on the line below, and turn this sheet in for teacher approval. Upon receiving approval, begin working on your poster, keeping in mind what you have learned about making good posters.

Subject area _____

Topic (personal choice) _____

Approval _____

Choose a different topic _____

Notes:

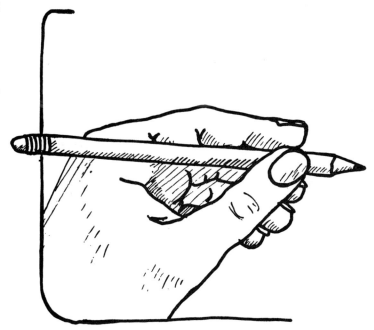

Due date for finished poster _____

ACTIVITY 17.
Charting Data

TEACHER PREVIEW

LESSON DESCRIPTIONS

Introductory Narrative ("The Numbers Game"): Susan describes an assignment from her science teacher that required her to subdivide a set of unorganized facts into groups and then to think of ways to present those facts visually by charting or graphing them.

Reading Material: The Data Sheet given to Susan and her classmates. This sheet contains forty-two unorganized facts about four completely different topics: the world's ten highest peaks; world population by continent; oil imports from Saudi Arabia; and Democratic and Republican votes in presidential elections, 1932–1984.

Classroom Assignment: In a class discussion, students identify the categories under which each of the facts should be grouped. (The four categories are listed above.) Then they brainstorm ways of presenting the facts in each category visually. Following the discussion, students record the categories and graphing or charting ideas on their assignment sheets. Then each student selects one category to actually graph or chart. Upon completing this assignment, students may be asked to present their work to the class.

Examples of Susan's graphs and charts are provided with this Teacher Preview. They may be used in a variety of ways, but it is suggested that they not be shown to students until *after* the Classroom Assignment is completed. Then the examples can be used for comparison and to help prepare students for the On Your Own assignment.

On Your Own: Each student chooses a topic, collects data, and produces a visual presentation of the facts that are collected. The topic must receive teacher approval, and the assignment sheet offers the option of requiring that a rough draft be handed in before a final chart or graph is begun.

SUGGESTIONS FOR SETTING THE STAGE

- Bring examples of charts and graphs from news magazines, newspapers, and other sources, to show how professionals organize information for visual presentation. Talk about how much easier it is to understand information that has been put into simple graph form.

• Bring a set of facts to class, and have students offer ideas for graphing or charting them. Then make a rough example of such a chart or graph on the chalkboard, on an overhead, or on a large piece of paper. Students may be asked to work on individual examples at their desks. An example is U.S. Defense Department expenditures from 1915 to the present. This information makes an interesting line graph, showing the dramatic increase in defense spending during this century. The data for this topic is recorded below if you wish to use it. Numbers are rounded to the nearest hundred million dollars. You may add recent figures if they are available.

U.S. Defense Outlays
in millions of dollars

1915	300	1960	44,000
1918	6,100	1965	47,200
1929	800	1970	78,400
1933	800	1975	87,500
1939	1,400	1980	136,100
1943	63,400	1983	207,900
1945	80,500	1984	223,900
1950	9,900	1985	244,100
1956	35,700	1986	273,400

Otto Johnson, et al., eds., *The 1988 Information Please Almanac*
(Boston: Houghton Mifflin Company, 1988), pp. 70–71.
SOURCE: Department of the Treasury, Financial Management Service

Susan's graphs and charts follow.

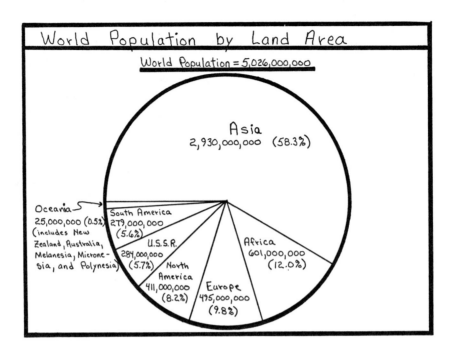

World Population by Land Area

World Population = 5,026,000,000

Asia
2,930,000,000 (58.3%)

Oceania
25,000,000 (0.5%)
(includes New
Zealand, Australia,
Melanesia, Microne-
sia, and Polynesia)

South America
279,000,000
(5.6%)

U.S.S.R.
284,000,000
(5.7%)

North
America
411,000,000
(8.2%)

Europe
495,000,000
(9.8%)

Africa
601,000,000
(12.0%)

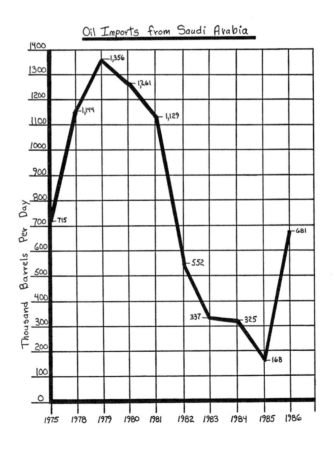

Oil Imports from Saudi Arabia

ACTIVITY 17. Charting Data

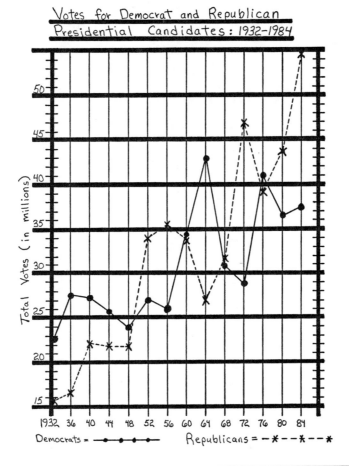

Votes for Democrat and Republican Presidential Candidates: 1932–1984

Democrats = ●——●——●
Republicans = –*––*––*

Mountain Peak	Range	Location	Height	
			feet	meters
The World's Ten Highest Peaks				
Everest	Himalayas	Nepal – Tibet	29,028	8,848
Godwin Austen	Karakoram	Kashmir	28,250	8,610
Kanchenjunga	Himalayas	Nepal – Sikkim	28,208	8,598
Lhotse	Himalayas	Nepal – Tibet	27,890	8,501
Makalu	Himalayas	Tibet – Nepal	27,790	8,470
Dhaulagiri 1	Himalayas	Nepal	26,810	8,172
Manaslu	Himalay s	Nepal	26,760	8,156
Cho Oyu	Himalayas	Nepal	26,750	8,153
Nanga Parbat	Himalayas	Kashmir	26,660	8,126
Annapurna 1	Himalayas	Nepal	26,504	8,078

Name _____ Date _____

INTRODUCTORY NARRATIVE

Read the following narrative to find out how Susan handled an assignment to chart information given to her on a data sheet.

The Numbers Game
by Susan

I've always wanted to be a scientist. Even when I was very small and could barely talk, my answer to the "what do you want to be when you grow up" question was a "tientist." I haven't lost that dream. In fact, I'm thinking about college and careers now, and I've decided I'd like to be a chemist or a physicist and specialize in the study of new materials, especially ceramics. I'd be called a materials scientist. Hey! Don't laugh until you've checked it out. Some day you'll realize that I'm right. The world of the future will be built of plastics, ceramics, and glass.

Anyway, the point of all this is that I take my science classes very seriously. Recently, my science teacher, Miss MacCauly, spent a full week explaining and demonstrating the importance of being able to chart (or graph) experimental or field data. She said one of the functions of a scientist is to make facts clear and understandable. She also emphasized that many careers place a premium on the ability to organize information by putting it into such visual forms as charts, tables, graphs, drawings, outlines, or illustrations. Some of the examples she gave were lab chemists, meteorologists, engineers, architects, anthropologists, medical researchers, business people, economists, astronomers, physicists, military planners, and lawyers. All these people need data in a form that can be used and shown to others. I realized during Miss MacCauly's unit on charting data that it was a skill I needed to perfect.

One of the projects we worked on in class was very interesting. We were given a data sheet that was filled with unorganized facts. We had to think of ways to put the information into a visual form, to make it more understandable and therefore more useful. I worked hard on this assignment, and I was proud of the results when I presented what I'd done to the class. Everyone, including Miss MacCauly, said that I did a good job. Now I'm going to apply what I've learned to my next project: this year's science fair.

Name _____   Date _____

READING MATERIAL

The most important part of charting data is grouping it and organizing it. Given a large number of unorganized facts, it is necessary to first of all recognize the categories into which the information can be placed. Once this is done, each fact can be assigned to a group with all other similar or related facts. This first step sets the stage for putting the information into graph form.

Below is the data sheet that was given to Susan and her classmates. Read it over carefully and think about how you would group the facts that are presented. Be prepared to discuss possible methods of charting or graphing the information to make it easier to see relationships, trends, and the facts themselves.

Data Sheet

— Mount Everest of the Himalayas (Nepal—Tibet) is 29,028 feet (8,848 meters) high, the world's highest peak.

— The population of Asia in 1986 was 2,930,000,000 people.

— The U.S. imported 715,000 barrels of oil per day from Saudi Arabia in 1975.

— In the 1932 presidential election, the Republican received 15,800,000 votes and the Democrat received 22,800,000.

— Mount Godwin Austen of the Karakoram (Kashmir) is 28,250 feet (8,610 meters) high.

— In the 1952 presidential election, the Republican received 33,900,000 votes and the Democrat received 27,300,000.

— The U.S. imported 168,000 barrels of oil per day from Saudi Arabia in 1985.

— Mount Manaslu of the Himalayas (Nepal) is 26,760 feet (8,156 meters) high.

— In the 1984 presidential election the Republican received 54,500,000 votes and the Democrat received 37,600,000.

— The population of Africa in 1986 was 601,000,000 people.

— In the 1940 presidential election the Republican received 22,300,000 votes and the Democrat received 27,200,000.

— In the 1972 presidential election the Republican received 47,200,000 votes and the Democrat received 29,200,000.

— The U.S. imported 1,261,000 barrels of oil per day from Saudi Arabia in 1980.

— Mount Annapurna of the Himalayas (Nepal) is 26,504 feet (8,078 meters) high, the world's tenth highest peak.

— The population of the world in 1986 was 5,026,000,000 people.

— In the 1960 presidential election the Republican received 34,100,000 votes and the Democrat received 34,200,000.

— Mount Makalu of the Himalayas (Tibet—Nepal) is 27,790 feet (8,470 meters) high.

— The U.S. imported 337,000 barrels of oil per day from Saudi Arabia in 1983.

— In the 1936 presidential election the Republican received 16,700,000 votes and the Democrat received 27,800,000.

— The U.S. imported 1,144,000 barrels of oil per day from Saudi Arabia in 1978.

READING MATERIAL, CONT'D

- The population of North America in 1986 was 411,000,000 people.
- Mount Cho Oyu of the Himalayas (Nepal) is 26,750 feet (8,153 meters) high.
- In the 1964 presidential election the Republican received 27,200,000 votes and the Democrat received 43,100,000.
- The U.S. imported 681,000 barrels of oil per day from Saudi Arabia in 1986.
- Mount Kanchenjunga of the Himalayas (Nepal–Sikkim) is 28,208 feet (8,598 meters) high.
- In the 1948 presidential election the Republican received 22,000,000 votes and the Democrat received 24,200,000.
- The population of the U.S.S.R. in 1986 was 284,000,000 people.
- The U.S. imported 1,356,000 barrels of oil per day from Saudi Arabia in 1979.
- In the 1980 presidential election the Republican received 43,900,000 votes and the Democrat received 36,500,000.
- In the 1944 presidential election the Republican received 22,000,000 votes and the Democrat received 25,600,000.
- Mount Nanga Parbat of the Himalayas (Kashmir) is 26,660 feet (8,126 meters) high.
- The population of Europe in 1986 was 495,000,000 people.
- Mount Lhotse of the Himalayas (Nepal–Tibet) is 27,890 feet (8,501 meters) high.
- The U.S. imported 1,129,000 barrels of oil per day from Saudi Arabia in 1981.
- In the 1976 presidential election the Republican received 39,100,000 votes and the Democrat received 40,800,000.
- The population of South America in 1986 was 279,000,000 people.
- The U.S. imported 552,000 barrels of oil per day from Saudi Arabia in 1982.
- In the 1956 presidential election the Republican received 35,600,000 votes and the Democrat received 26,000,000.
- In the 1968 presidential election the Republican received 31,800,000 votes and the Democrat received 31,300,000.
- The U.S. imported 325,000 barrels of oil per day from Saudi Arabia in 1984.
- Mount Dhaulagiri of the Himalayas (Nepal) is 26,810 feet (8,172 meters) high.
- The population of Oceania (Australia, New Zealand, Melanesia, Micronesia, and Polynesia) in 1986 was 25,000,000 people.

All facts were taken from Otto Johnson et al., eds., *The 1988 Information Please Almanac* (Boston: Houghton Mifflin Company, 1988); "Crude Oil Imports & Petroleum Products . . . ," p. 387

SOURCE: 1975—U.S. Dept. of the Interior, Bureau of Mines; 1976 through 1986—U.S. Dept. of Energy, Energy Information Administration.

"World Population . . . ," p. 465

SOURCE: Population Reference Bureau, Inc.

"Highest Mountain Peaks of the World," p. 468

"Presidential Elections," pp. 614–615

Name ———————————— Date ————————————

CLASSROOM ASSIGNMENT

As a class, decide how to categorize the information on the Data Sheet and discuss ways of presenting it in a graph or chart. Following this discussion, fill in the worksheet below and choose *one* category to graph or chart. Make your graph or chart carefully, accurately, and neatly, and be prepared to present it to the class.

Categories	**Graphing or Charting Ideas**
1. ————————————	————————————
	————————————
	————————————
	————————————
2. ————————————	————————————
	————————————
	————————————
	————————————
3. ————————————	————————————
	————————————
	————————————
	————————————
4. ————————————	————————————
	————————————
	————————————
	————————————

Name _____ Date _____

ON YOUR OWN

Choose a topic about which you can collect enough data to make an informative chart or graph. Use almanacs, encyclopedias, newspapers, magazines, books, or your own research as sources of information. Record your topic below, along with your ideas about charting or graphing the data. Your teacher must approve the topic, and you may be asked to submit a rough draft of the visual display.

   The categories previously discussed are examples of topics you might choose. Of course, there are many others, such as temperature extremes in various states, the defense budget over the past few years (perhaps compared to the budget for social programs during the same years), population statistics, sports statistics, or results of your own polls or experiments. Methods of presenting information include illustrations, tables, line graphs, bar graphs, pie graphs, and organized lists.

Topic _____

Approval _____

Choose a different topic _____

Notes:

Rough draft due date _____

Rough draft approval _____

Rough draft needs more work _____

Notes:

Final chart or graph due date _____

ACTIVITY 18.
Expressing Ideas in an Editorial

TEACHER PREVIEW

LESSON DESCRIPTIONS

Introductory Narrative ("In My Opinion"): Cara explains how she became the editor of her school newspaper and why she immediately had to deal with a freedom of the press issue.

Reading Material: Cara's editorial about freedom of speech in the school paper. Students are told to be ready to discuss the editorial and to decide if they agree or disagree with Cara's point of view.

Classroom Assignment: Students search through materials you bring to class, looking for editorials. Each student chooses one editorial, cuts it out, underlines the important ideas, and explains in his or her own words what the central theme, idea, argument, or point of the editorial is. Finally, the students tells why he or she agrees or disagrees with the author. The editorial is attached to the assignment sheet and they are turned in. Some ideas for collecting sources of editorials:

* Assign students to bring newspapers and magazines from home.

* Ask a local newspaper to provide one copy per student of one day's edition.

* Save your own newspapers and magazines to bring in.

* Choose two or three editorials that can be copied and used by all students.

On Your Own: Each student chooses a topic and outlines ideas for an editorial. After receiving approval, he or she writes the editorial and turns it in on a specified date.

SUGGESTIONS FOR SETTING THE STAGE

* Bring an editorial from a local newspaper to class. Try to find one that talks about a topic of general interest to students or one in which they might become interested if introduced to it. Read it to the class and analyze it. Do students agree with what was said? Talk about the purpose of an editorial: who writes them, and why.

* Give the class a hypothetical situation and have students write brief editorials stating their opinions. For example, you might tell them to imagine how they would react if told that a new law decreed that only students with 3.0 grade point averages be allowed to complete the eleventh and twelfth grades. All others would be given a diploma for finishing the tenth grade and then assigned to either a job or a trade school for the next two years. Of course, only high school graduates would be allowed into college. Have each student pretend to be the editor of a newspaper and respond to this idea.

Name _____   Date _____

INTRODUCTORY NARRATIVE

Read the following narrative to understand how Cara became editor of her school newspaper after another student quit in anger when the principal told him to rewrite an editorial.

In My Opinion
by Cara

In January, 1988, the U.S. Supreme Court ruled that public school officials have the power to suppress controversial stories and editorials in student newspapers.* Justice Byron White wrote that "A school need not tolerate student speech that is inconsistent with its basic educational mission. School officials may impose reasonable restrictions on the speech of students, teachers and other members of the school community." When the former editor of our school newspaper was told to rewrite an editorial about AIDS, he accused the principal, Mrs. Watson, of violating his constitutional rights. Mrs. Watson responded by reading the above quote to him. She said, in effect, that the constitution does not extend complete, unbridled freedom to the pen of a student editor; that a principal in fact *does* have the power to control what goes into a student newspaper.

Well, the former editor, Tom, became quite agitated and angry. He refused to rewrite his article, and he threatened to quit the newspaper and drop the journalism class. When Mrs. Watson said "Fine," he stormed out of her office in a huff. He carried out his pledge to quit, and he pouted around school for at least two weeks. Tom is the kind of person who can't stand being told what to do, and he always has to have his own way. It was very hard on him to have his will thwarted, but Mrs. Watson seemed unaffected by his behavior. Within hours of receiving Tom's written request to drop the class, she contacted our journalism teacher Mr. Whiting, and instructed him to assign a new person to the job of student editor.

That's where I come in. Mr. Whiting asked me to be the new editor. I accepted, even though Tom tried to pressure me and the rest of the students to quit with him. None of us did. We like journalism, and it made more sense to learn to live with reality. My dad told me that you can't argue with a Supreme Court ruling. He said that you become completely ineffective if you quit, so the only sensible option is learn the rules of the game and play by them. It sounded like such good advice that I've taken it as my personal motto: don't quit; learn to play the game.

My first assignment as student editor was to write an editorial for the upcoming issue of the newspaper. I chose to write about freedom of the press, constitutional rights, and student newspapers. The whole school knew about the confrontation between Tom and Mrs. Watson, and there was some polarizing of opinions. It was important to state publicly how the new editor felt about these issues and to speak for the entire journalism class in explaining how controversial topics that may be subject to administrative censorship would be handled. I think I did a pretty good job of dealing with the situation, and I learned a lot about the power of the press, the power of the law, and the power of Mrs. Watson. The greatest lesson was realizing the importance of learning to live within the boundaries of what is possible. My dad calls it pragmatism and realpolitik. After looking these words up, I'd say I agree.

*Hazelwood School District v. Kuhlmeier, 484 U.S. 260(1988)

Name _____   Date _____

READING MATERIAL

Editorials are a way for a newspaper or magazine to express the opinions of the people who write and publish it. They come from individual, personal points of view, and they are generally written to convince a reader of the correctness of an idea or, in the negative sense, of the incorrectness of someone else's idea. Occasionally editorials present straight, unbiased facts, but usually they offer opinions, ideas, stands on issues, and philosophies, supported by facts as they are needed. Doing the necessary research and acknowledging other viewpoints are two important components of an editorial.

Below is the editorial Cara wrote about student rights and freedom of the press. She meant to express her own opinions while simultaneously speaking for the newspaper staff as a whole. Her audience wanted to know what was going on, so she was writing an explanation of the relationship between the principal and the student editor, and of the role a school newspaper should play. Read the editorial carefully. Be prepared to discuss it in class, to decide if Cara did a good job of presenting her case. Also, be ready to tell if you agree or disagree with her point of view and the way she handled the whole situation.

Freedom of Speech and Student Journalists:
Where We Stand
by Cara Otten

Living in America, we take our freedoms for granted. We live in a country that has a written guarantee against tyranny and abuse of power. The constitution has protected individuals for over two hundred years while it has preserved our rights as citizens of a free nation. Our notion of "freedom" is so ingrained into our way of thinking, in fact, that we sometimes assume we have rights which we really don't have. Such is apparently the case with freedom of the press within a public school.

Recently the editor of *The Flyer* resigned his position in a dispute with the administration over freedom of speech. He wrote an editorial about AIDS which Mrs. Watson did not want published. She asked him to rewrite it, and he refused, citing his constitutional right to freedom of speech. He was told that student editors and school newspapers have no such right, and he resigned in protest. Now, with a new editor in place, the question arises: where do we stand and how do we proceed?

There was good reason for believing that freedom of speech applied to students and school newspapers. The first amendment to the constitution, ratified in 1791, states: "Congress shall make no law respecting an establishment of religion, or prohibiting the free exercise thereof; or abridging the freedom of speech, or of the press; . . ." In the 1969 Supreme Court case *Tinker v. Des Moines Independent Community School District* the question was: can students wear black armbands in class to protest the war in Vietnam? Justice Abe Fortas wrote in the decision that students do not "shed their constitutional rights to freedom of speech or expression at the schoolhouse gate." This would lead you to believe that school newspapers are free and independent. Not so.

In 1988 the Supreme Court decided another case, *Hazelwood School District v. Kuhlmeier,* in which it ruled that school officials have the right to determine what is published in a school newspaper. This is the final word. Principals, superintendents, and school boards may ban any

READING MATERIAL, CONT'D

story they wish, using their own standards to make the decision. The Supreme Court has spoken, and that's the law of the land.

The staff of *The Flyer* believes the situation calls for pragmatism and realpolitik. In other words, we must face the real world and live with things we can't change. It is true that we have a censor, but it is also true that she has always tried to be fair and has seldom used her veto power. We are certain we can work with Mrs. Watson to ensure that all of our stories, columns, and editorials are published. We do not feel repressed or controlled, but we are aware of the power that Mrs. Watson wields. If there is something written that the administration definitely does not want published, it won't be: that's the bottom line. We trust Mrs. Watson to use good judgement in deciding what is not publishable and that her standards will be based on what is truly poor taste, harmful to others, or bad journalism rather than on what is displeasing to the administration.

As the new editor, I had a meeting with Mrs. Watson to discuss the issue of censorship and freedom of speech. During that meeting we came up with five ideas for assuring as much freedom as possible. I'm printing them here for all to see, because this is how *The Flyer* will operate from now on.

- Every article will undergo a four point test to decide if it is publishable. This test asks whether the article is accurate, tasteful, discreet, and unbiased.

- We have moved the deadline for articles up three days to allow more proofreading and rewriting time. Articles will be submitted to Mr. Whiting, who will pass them on to Mrs. Watson. Mrs. Watson has agreed to read the entire paper in its manuscript or rough draft form, something she's never done before.

- If an article is banned, *The Flyer* will run a story explaining what the topic was and who wrote the banned article.

- Every time Mrs. Watson vetoes an article submission she will write a brief explanation of her reasons, for publication in *The Flyer*.

- If the editor *and* the journalism adviser (Mr. Whiting) both disagree with the principal's decision to ban an article, an appeal may be made to the superintendent of instruction, whose word is final.

I think this is a fair arrangement that gives the principal the control she needs without stepping all over our rights. What I think about having a limit on our student press doesn't matter. It's there as a result of a Supreme Court ruling. That fact cannot be changed; we have to live with it. Our readers will still receive all the school news and more, just as before.

Name _____   Date _____

CLASSROOM ASSIGNMENT

Search through the materials that are provided in the classroom and find an editorial that interests you. Read it carefully and then follow the assignment below.

1. If the editorial is in a magazine or newspaper, cut it out before beginning the lesson.

2. Underline what you consider to be the important points the author was trying to make in the editorial.

3. Record what you think is the author's central theme, idea, argument, or point. Write this in your own words, as if you were explaining it to a friend.

4. Explain briefly why you agree or disagree with the author's point of view. If you don't really care one way or another, explain why the author didn't bring you around to his or her way of thinking.

5. Attach the editorial to this assignment sheet and turn it in when it is completed.

Author's central theme, idea, argument, or point:

Your opinion about the editorial and the point of view it expresses:

Name _____ **Date** _____

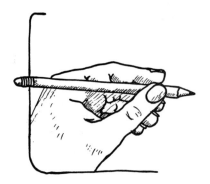

ON YOUR OWN

Choose a topic about which you could write an editorial (or personal opinion article), either because you have strong feelings or because you know a lot about the subject. On the lines below record the topic, the main points you would make, and a heading or title for such an editorial. Turn this assignment sheet in, and when it is returned with teacher approval, write the editorial just as you would if it were being published. The due date for the finished editorial should also be recorded below.

Topic: _____

Main points: _____

_____

_____

_____

_____

_____

_____

_____

_____

_____

_____

_____

Heading or title: _____

Teacher approval _____ Comments:

Topic needs more work _____

Choose a new topic _____

Due date _____

ACTIVITY 19.
Describing Action

TEACHER PREVIEW

LESSON DESCRIPTIONS

Introductory Narrative ("Words of a Master: Stephen Crane"): Joshua tells about his introduction to Stephen Crane's work and how that discovery led him to try his hand at describing action.

Reading Material: An explanation of what it means to write in the "active voice," followed by excerpts from *The Red Badge of Courage* which illustrate how Stephen Crane described action.

Classroom Assignment: Each student chooses a situation from a list that is provided and writes a one-paragraph description of the action that might take place.

On Your Own: Each student chooses a situation from a list of twenty (ten from the Classroom Assignment and ten more on this assignment sheet) and writes a two-page (minimum) description of the action that might take place.

SUGGESTIONS FOR SETTING THE STAGE

- Bring a collection of novels and short stories to class, or conduct this activity in a library. Be sure the authors of the books you select specialize in describing action: ask your librarian for suggestions. Have students browse through one or two books, looking for passages that vividly describe action. Have them read some of the passages aloud in class, and discuss the quality and style of the writing.

- Write a sentence on the board and tell each student to rewrite it, using colorful, descriptive, and dynamic words and phrases to create a mental picture of the action. Have students read their rewritten sentences to the class and discuss them, placing emphasis on the importance of using strong, active verbs and descriptive adverbs. Explain that action writing includes descriptions of how characters *feel, think,* and *behave,* as well as environmental factors and the actual action that takes place. Here are some sample sentences that may be used:

– The Sun was hot as the man walked across the desert.

– The woman dropped her purse when the thief told her to.

– The car was hit from behind by a bus.

– The child was afraid when the closet door opened.

– The elephants ran through the jungle.

• Give the class a series of ideas for sentences that show action, and have students list verbs, adverbs, or phrases that could be used to give these sentences clarity or descriptive power. Put one idea at a time on the board, and then allow students to write for sixty seconds. After several ideas are done, discuss each by asking students for their suggestions and recording them on the board. Compose "class sentences" (or "class paragraphs"), using verbs, adverbs, and phrases from various students to illustrate creative description of action scenes. Here are some sample ideas:

– a fall from a cliff	– a shark hunting for food
– a tornado touching down	– a rocket at liftoff
– a ride in a hang glider	– a headache
– a dive into ice-cold water	– a ride on a roller coaster
– a temper tantrum	– a fireworks display

Name _____   Date _____

INTRODUCTORY NARRATIVE

Read the following narrative to learn how Joshua became interested in writing fiction while working on a literature assignment.

Words of a Master: Stephen Crane
by Joshua

I've always loved to read, but writing never excited me much. I guess I thought that to be a good writer you had to have a deep philosophical message, or else you had to be a great storyteller. Now I've discovered another avenue for creative writing, one which doesn't require me to be a Herman Melville or a Henry David Thoreau or a Mark Twain. My newfound passion for writing comes from learning to describe action. I love to write about conflict, adventure, and the forces of nature at work. To me, describing the action on the line of scrimmage in a football game or picturing (in words) the violence of an erupting volcano is more enjoyable than composing an essay or writing a story. Because of my interest in learning to describe action, I've been doing more composition lately. It's fun to see improvement in myself and to realize that I *do* have writing ability.

I give credit to one person for my sudden and fervent desire to write. Born in 1871, he wrote (among other things) a book about the Civil War, *the Red Badge of Courage*. His name is Stephen Crane, and I was introduced to his work almost by accident. Mrs. Evans, my literature teacher, taught a unit on authors who specialize in describing action. Each student chose one author from a long list and located excerpts of that person's writing to read to the class. These examples introduced us to a variety of writing styles. Mrs. Evans placed great emphasis on the authors' use of the active voice in their writing. She pointed out that good writers almost never use the passive voice.

Anyway, I chose Stephen Crane and read *The Red Badge of Courage*. Almost the entire story is an example of action writing. I enjoyed it so much that I read it a second time right away. I chose some excellent excerpts to read to the class and everyone agreed that Stephen Crane did an extraordinary job of describing action. More than that, he convinced me to try my hand at writing.

Name _____   Date _____

READING MATERIAL

One of the keys to good writing is the use of the active voice. *Voice* is a grammatical term used to tell if the subject of a sentence is acting or is receiving the action described by the verb. If it acts it is called the *doer;* if it receives the action it is called the *receiver.* For example:

John hit the ball. (John is the subject and the *doer* of the action.)

The ball was hit by John. (Ball is the subject and the *receiver* of the action.)

The first sentence is written in the active voice, and second sentence is written in the passive voice. The active voice means the subject does something; it is the *doer* of the action. This is the preferable form for most writing.

An idea cannot be expressed in the passive voice without combining a form of the verb *to be* (am, are, is, was, were, will be, shall be, have been, etc.) with the past participle of a principal verb. If you find yourself using such verb forms often in your writing, you are probably a passive writer. Try to think of ways to have the subjects of your sentences do the action and you will find yourself writing in the active voice.

Below are the excerpts Joshua chose from Stephen Crane's Civil War story, *The Red Badge of Courage.** Read them over to see how a master writer uses active verbs.

1. The battle flag in the distance jerked about madly. It seemed to be struggling to free itself from an agony. The billowing smoke was filled with horizontal flashes. Men running swiftly emerged from it. They grew in numbers until it was seen that the whole command was fleeing. The flag suddenly sank down as if dying. Its motion as it fell was a gesture of despair. Wild yells came from behind the walls of smoke. A sketch in gray and red dissolved into a moblike body of men who galloped like wild horses.

2. As he, leading, went across a little field, he found himself in a region of shells. They hurtled over his head with long wild screams. As he listened he imagined them to have rows of cruel teeth that grinned at him. Once one lit before him and the livid lightning of the explosion effectually barred the way in his chosen direction. He groveled on the ground and then springing up went careering off through some bushes.

3. The flames bit him, and the hot smoke broiled his skin. His rifle barrel grew so hot that ordinarily he could not have borne it upon his palms; but he kept on stuffing cartridges into it, and pounding them with his clanking, bending ramrod. If he aimed at some changing form through the smoke, he pulled his trigger with a fierce grunt, as if he were dealing a blow of the fist with all his strength.

*Stephen Crane, *The Red Badge of Courage,* Washington Square Press, Inc., 1965, pp. 34, 47, 112.

Name _____ Date _____

CLASSROOM ASSIGNMENT

Choose one of the situations listed below and write a one-paragraph description of the action that takes place. Make every effort to write in the active voice, and try to be as descriptive as possible. Be prepared to read your paragraph to the class. You may also be asked to hand the paragraph in for evaluation.

    I have decided to write about situation no. _____

SITUATIONS

1. Describe the actions of a person who has just hit his or her thumb with a hammer.
2. Describe the scene in the living room of a person who has just realized that he or she has won a million dollar lottery.
3. Describe the feeling or action of being chased in a dream.
4. Describe the motions of a ballet dancer.
5. Describe how an eagle looks (or what it experiences) as it soars high above the ground.
6. Describe the moment when a person realizes that he or she has forgotten to do a major assignment that is due today.
7. Describe the actions of an athlete in the final moments of a close contest when he or she makes the winning (or losing) shot, play, move, or effort.
8. Describe the scene on a stage as a popular musician finishes an encore before an appreciative audience.
9. Describe the action between a predator and its prey at the moment of attack (for example, between a lion and an antelope or an owl and a mouse).
10. Describe a situation of your own. Record the situation below, and ask for teacher approval before beginning.

    Situation: _____

_____

_____

_____

_____

_____

_____

_____

    Teacher approval: _____

Name _____ **Date** _____

ON YOUR OWN

Choose a situation from the list below and describe an action scene as if it were part of a short story or novel you are writing. A brief one- or two-sentence introduction is all that is necessary to set the stage for the action. The reader should get a clear picture of the action that is taking place but need not understand the rest of the story. Your action scene should be a detailed and descriptive account of the situation you choose. Its minimum length is two handwritten pages.

I have decided to write about situation no. _____

Due date _____

Situations

1–9. See the Classroom Assignment sheet.
10. Describe the reaction of an astronaut who discovers that returning to Earth may be impossible because of a rocket malfunction.
11. Describe an Old West shootout in the streets of a western town.
12. Describe a ride on the most terrifying (or exciting) amusement park ride you have ever ridden.
13. Describe a bicycle chase scene in which a "good guy" is being chased by a "bad guy" through the streets and alleys of a town or city.
14. Describe a group of kids entering and exploring a "haunted house."
15. Describe the experience of a person who is stuck in a blizzard and must walk to find help.
16. Describe a thunderstorm.
17. Describe an earthquake.
18. Describe what happens when a person is trapped on the twentieth floor of a burning hotel.
19. Describe the plight of an animal (a deer or, for example a rabbit) caught in a forest fire.
20. Describe a situation of your own. Record the situation below, and ask for teacher approval before beginning.

Situation: _____

_____

_____

_____

_____

Teacher approval: _____

Comments:

ACTIVITY 20.
Preparing a Résumé

TEACHER PREVIEW

LESSON DESCRIPTIONS

Introductory Narrative ("You Are What You Write"): Russell tells about his attempt to get a work-study job in the advertising or public relations department of a large company. His application was rejected because he failed to take the time to learn how to prepare a proper résumé.

Reading Material: Suggestions for writing good résumés, followed by two examples of Russell's résumé. The first example is a copy of the résumé Russell sent with his job application, and the second is what he wrote after he learned how a résumé should be organized.

Classroom Assignment: Students are given a description of an imaginary company (Consolidated Products Corp.) that is moving into their community, along with a list of positions that the company must fill for its new plant. Each student invents or creates a person who is applying for one of the positions and writes a résumé for that person. Samples and reference materials should be available for students to study.

On Your Own: Each student writes his or her own personal résumé.

SUGGESTIONS FOR SETTING THE STAGE

- Tell the class that a hypothetical job opportunity for high school students has just become available and that it requires a résumé. Instruct each person to make a list of the things he or she would include in a personal résumé and set a time limit of about ten minutes for students to make their lists. Then in a class discussion ask students to read some of the things they listed. Talk about the value and appropriateness of each item. Explain what an employer is looking for in a well written résumé and why résumés are necessary at all. This activity will help prepare students for the "On Your Own" lesson.

- Have students search through the classified ads of newspapers you (and they) bring to class, looking for help wanted notices and circling the ones that might require résumés. Discuss the time in the near future when they will probably be faced with the reality of competing for good jobs and point out some of the things that help ensure actually landing one—education, references, résumé, appearance, and interviewing skills. This activity will help students realize what kinds of jobs are available in their community and should lead to a better understanding of how to prepare for entering the job market.

- Ask local companies for written guidelines or suggestions that they give job applicants who wish to submit résumés to them, so that students can see what the companies are looking for in a résumé. If possible, ask a hiring officer or personnel administrator to talk to your class.

Name ———————————————— Date ————————————————

INTRODUCTORY NARRATIVE

Read the following narrative to learn how Russell came to realize that the ability to write a résumé is an important skill.

You Are What You Write
by Russell

I've always been pretty good at getting what I want. I'm not devious or anything; just persistent. My parents know that if I set my mind on something there's no talking me out of it: I've been that way all my life. When I managed to be assigned to drive the queen's car and be her escort in this year's homecoming parade and then got a date with the queen (just as I predicted I would), even my friends believed in my power to pull off the impossible. They started calling me "Can-do," as in, "He can do anything." Well, I guess I let it go to my head and I became a little too confident in my ability to make things happen according to my own plans. I thought I was something special, and for that reason I could have anything if I just decided I wanted it. Arrogant? Conceited? Yes, I admit it. My father told me so. He said I was becoming a "stuffed shirt."

Recently, I got taken down a couple of notches when I set my sights on a work-study job and my application was rejected. I thought that because of who I am, my past successes, and my natural abilities, the job was in my pocket. *Wrong!* The selection was based solely on the quality of the résumé and the qualifications of the candidate. Instead of learning how to write a résumé, I just wrote an annotated outline explaining why I deserved the job. I don't think I was ever in contention, and it may have even been taken as a joke, because what I wrote wasn't a résumé at all. Looking back, I realize that I learned an important lesson: it's good to have confidence, but confidence should lead to quality, not snobbery. My dad was right about me becoming a stuffed shirt, and I'm glad to put an end to that phase of my life.

The usefulness of writing a proper résumé was not lost on me, either. I have since learned what a good résumé should look like, and the next opportunity that comes along will find me prepared with the skills I need to do the job right. Writing résumés, interviewing for jobs, organizing my ideas for presentation to others—these are things I will do in the future which will have real consequences in my life. It has finally dawned on me that I should prepare for that time *now*, so when the time comes, I'll be ready. That's not conceit; it's just plain, common sense.

Name _____   Date _____

READING MATERIAL

NOTES: A résumé is a convenient way of telling a potential employer about your education and work experiences. There are many ways to organize a résumé and numerous books and pamphlets are available that give specific details, examples, and suggestions. Most authors, teachers, and people in the business community agree that there are some basic things to keep in mind when preparing a résumé. Three cardinal rules are: be brief (one typewritten page); be simple and straightforward; be honest. Follow these rules and you will produce a useful résumé.

There are, of course, other considerations to think about when preparing a résumé. A résumé should be typed—single spaced, with double spaces between sections. It should be concisely written so that it can be read quickly and easily. Employers are not interested in unnecessary or irrelevant information such as height, weight, sex, hobbies, personal beliefs, likes and dislikes, and so forth; don't clutter a résumé with such things. While trying to be concise, you must also include enough details to give a clear picture of job experiences and educational background. This is perhaps the most difficult part of writing a résumé: clarity combined with brevity. Another important factor in résumé writing is organization. Headings and subheadings should be used so that information is easy to find. Finally, be sure to proofread a completed résumé, and ask someone else to proofread it, too. Never send out a résumé that has misspellings, typographical errors, poor grammar, or improperly written sentences. You are trying to project an image of competence; correct writing is essential to that goal.

When the résumé is sent to a prospective employer, include a cover letter that clearly explains why you decided to apply to that particular organization. If the letter shows that you understand what a business does and what its needs are, you are more likely to be taken seriously by the person who makes hiring decisions. Follow the three cardinal rules of brevity, simplicity and honesty for the cover letter, and be persistent! Keep trying until you succeed. There are doors just waiting to open to the person who has the right key. In many cases the key is a well-written résumé and cover letter.

READING MATERIAL, CONT'D

Example 1: Russell's Original Résumé

RESUME: A QUALIFIED PERSON FOR AN IMPORTANT JOB

Name: Russell C. ("Can-do") Forester   Grade: 11   Wt: 165 lbs.
        538 Vincent St.   Age: 17   Sex: M
        Bigtown, MI 49503   Ht:5'10"   Eyes: brown
Phone: (616)555-3883   Hair: black

Best trait: A burning desire to succeed; to be the best.
Worst trait: Tendency to be a perfectionist; although this leads to
             quality, it can be irritating.

    Let me start off by saying that this work-study program is a
valuable opportunity for young adults like me who are struggling to
make a start in life. Speaking for all students who hope to benefit
from the jobs you are offering, I thank you. I hope you realize,
however, that you will benefit, too. I am energetic, punctual,
reliable, creative, articulate, ambitious, and well educated, all
traits which would allow me to carry out the requirements of the job
with quality and verve.
    Now, a description of Russell C. Forester, the potential and
future employee:

Education: I have gone to school here in Bigtown my entire life. My
               teachers have all liked me and I've always gotten good
               grades. My current G.P.A. is 3.62, in spite of the
               difficulty of the classes I choose to take. I am a member
               of the National Honor Society, and I've been on an
               award-winning debate team for two years.

Work: I've held several positions over the years, and they
               are listed below. It should be noted that my most
               challenging job is the most recent one (at the grocery
               store), where I am head of a department with three
               younger workers under me.

               * newspaper deliverer   * snow removal business
               * lawn maintenance   * grocery bagging and
                 service   restocking.

Extracurricular Activities:
               I'm involved in many after-school, evening, weekend
               and summer activities. I'm on the wrestling team
               (healthy body/healthy mind); I'm active in my church;
               I play trombone in the band; I have a part-time job (see
               above); I belong to the camera club, and I like to hang
               glide.

References: I have attached a list of references that may be
               contacted to inquire about my qualifications. These
               twenty people know me and have worked with me in some
               way during the past few years. Each one can provide
               evidence that I am a good candidate for this position.

READING MATERIAL, CONT'D

Example 2: Russell's Revised Résumé

RUSSELL C. FORESTER
538 Vincent St.
Bigtown, MI 49503
(616)555-3883

Job Target: Work-Study in Advertising or Public Relations

CAPABILITIES (I can):

— Type 45 words per minute
— Take photographs and work in a darkroom
— Work with computers
— Write in proper English
— Perform simple office chores
— Assist in organizing or developing ideas
— Be responsible for all assigned tasks
— Learn new skills

ACHIEVEMENTS:

— I have published several articles in our school newspaper.
— I have received three awards for participating in competitions
  as a member of the debate team.
— I am a member of the National Honor Society.
— My current grade point average is 3.62.
— I earned the right to work on an independent project in my
  computer class.

WORK EXPERIENCE:

— Newspaper deliverer (3 years)
— Stock boy and grocery bagger at Morton's Supermarket (1 year)
— Staff writer for school newspaper (6 months)

EDUCATION:

— Junior at Bigtown High School
— Enrolled in college preparation curriculum
— Member of the debate team
— Currently taking chemistry, journalism, history, computers,
  and honors English

Name _____ Date _____

CLASSROOM ASSIGNMENT

Read the description below of an imaginary company that is moving into your community. Then develop a résumé for a person who is applying for one of the positions listed. This person is someone you will invent, and his or her credentials are left entirely up to you. Your responsibility is to produce a concise, well-written résumé for the person you create, based upon what you have learned about writing résumés from this activity and from class discussions. Write the résumé in your neatest handwriting on lined paper.

Consolidated Products Corporation

This company is a pioneer in the development of new materials, especially plastics and ceramics. It also manufactures products made of these new materials. The CONSOLIDATED motto is "It's already the twenty-first century at Consolidated Products." When this company moves into town, it will hire over 100 people, and some of the positions are described below. They are mostly in research and development, but some are also in sales, advertising, maintenance, security, and production. The company places a high premium on people who are qualified, motivated, loyal, and independent thinkers.

Position	Description
Physicist:	Work on developing ceramic superconductors.
Chemist:	Work on developing biodegradable and recyclable plastics.
Engineer:	Test products made of new materials.
Advertising executive:	Develop strategies for selling new products, especially overseas.
Sales manager:	Organize distribution of products to other companies through sales representatives.
Security specialist:	Protect trade secrets from theft by competitors.
Production expert:	Develop ways of manufacturing new products quickly and efficiently.
Executive secretary:	Organize filing and record-keeping systems; maintain office schedules; other secretarial duties.

Name ———————————————— Date ————————————————

ON YOUR OWN

It is a good idea to learn how to write a résumé before entering the job market for the first time, and that is why high school students should spend time preparing their own résumés. The experience is good practice for future job hunting activities; at the same time a well-written résumé might come in handy right away. You never know when an opportunity might arise, and the person who anticipates opportunities is more likely to succeed than the one who simply reacts to events after they happen. Preparation is a key to success.

For this lesson you will prepare your own personal résumé. There are three basic kinds of résumés:

- Time-line résumé, which lists work experience in reverse order. The most recent experience should be listed first.
- Personal qualifications résumé, which focuses on areas of ability and potential rather than work history.
- Focused résumé, which focuses on a specific job target and features statements of what you can do: your capabilities that make you a good candidate for the job.

Assignment

Prepare your own personal résumé, typed if possible, but if not, written in your neatest handwriting. A typed résumé should be one page long, and no more. Spend some time thinking about what format to use and what information to include before beginning. If there is a specific job right now that you would like to apply for, use the focused résumé format; otherwise, use one of the other two formats.

Your completed résumé is due on this date: ————————————————

ACTIVITY 21.
Producing an Oral Presentation

TEACHER PREVIEW

LESSON DESCRIPTIONS

Introductory Narrative ("A Picture and a Thousand Words"): Erin describes a camera club activity which required her to produce an oral presentation to be given at a photography exhibit in a local mall. She explains how the club's adviser prepared the members to make such presentations.

Reading Material: An information sheet that summarizes what a person must do to prepare for an oral presentation.

Classroom Assignment: Students develop materials that are designed to help younger students prepare to make oral presentations. Each student chooses *one* of three separate assignments to work on:

- An "Oral Presentation Evaluation Sheet" which itemizes the things that a teacher would grade in an oral presentation.

- An "Oral Presentation Checklist" which lists things a student should think about and have finished before giving an oral presentation.

- A "Suggestions and Advice Sheet" which lists things a student should consider, prepare for, or do before starting an oral presentation project.

On Your Own: Each student prepares an oral presentation about a personally chosen topic from a subject area assigned by you (to go along with your regular curriculum). These presentations are to be given, one per day, for a period of five to six weeks, and each one is to last no more than ten minutes. Volunteers are asked to go first (the order is determined by a drawing), and the first five presenters are given a five point bonus to compensate for less preparation time and for being models for the rest of the class to follow. An "Oral Presentation Evaluation Sheet" is provided for you to use with this project.

SUGGESTIONS FOR SETTING THE STAGE

- In a class discussion, list all of the occupations that students can think of that require oral presentation skills. Encourage students to think of all possibilities, even jobs that include talking to very small groups or involve one-on-one discussions. Also, ask students to think of jobs for which oral presentation skills might not be necessary, but where they would be helpful.

- In a class discussion, list topics that could be used for oral presentations for the On Your Own lesson in this activity. These topics should all relate to a subject area that fits into your curriculum. Remember that one presentation is made each day: the first presenter should have at least two weeks for preparation after the assignment is made, and presentations will continue about six weeks thereafter. Topics should focus on a subject being covered during this time period.

- Demonstrate or discuss a variety of visual materials that can be used in conjunction with an oral presentation. Perhaps a media specialist or art consultant could make a special presentation to your class. Mention such things as posters, overhead transparencies, chalkboard, slides, filmstrips, handouts or information sheets, videotapes, displays, and demonstrations.

Name _____ Date _____

ORAL PRESENTATION EVALUATION

This form shows how your oral presentation has been evaluated. It indicates areas where improvement is needed and where you have done well.

Topic _____

I. Presentation (50 points possible)
   A. Eye contact .... 3 pts. ____
   B. Voice projection .... 3 pts. ____
   C. Use of the English language .... 3 pts. ____
   D. Inflection .... 3 pts. ____
   E. Articulation .... 3 pts. ____
   F. Posture .... 3 pts. ____
   G. Use of hands .... 3 pts. ____
   H. Appropriate vocabulary .... 3 pts. ____
   I. Accurate information .... 10 pts. ____
   J. Information is easy to understand .... 3 pts. ____
   K. Enough information .... 3 pts. ____
   L. Information relates to topic .... 3 pts. ____
   M. Effort .... 7 pts. ____
   Subtotal ____

II. Visual or Extra Materials (30 points possible)
   A. Information is easy to understand .... 3 pts. ____
   B. Information relates to the oral report .... 3 pts. ____
   C. Information is current .... 3 pts. ____
   D. Information is accurate .... 3 pts. ____
   E. Enough information .... 3 pts. ____
   F. Neatness .... 3 pts. ____
   G. Spelling .... 3 pts. ____
   H. Artistic effort .... 3 pts. ____
   I. Research effort .... 3 pts. ____
   J. Appropriate vocabulary .... 3 pts. ____
   Subtotal ____

III. Question-Answer Period (20 points possible)
   A. Confidence in knowledge of topic .... 3 pts. ____
   B. Ability to answer reasonable questions .... 3 pts. ____
   C. Answers are accurate. .... 3 pts. ____
   D. Student is willing to admit limits of knowledge or under-
      standing. .... 2 pts. ____
   E. Answers are brief. .... 3 pts. ____
   F. Student exhibits ability to infer or hypothesize an answer
      from available information. .... 3 pts. ____
   G. Student appears to have put effort into learning about this
      topic. .... 3 pts. ____
   Subtotal ____
   TOTAL (100 pts. possible) _____

   Bonus (first five presenters only)
COMMENTS: 5 pts. ____

Name ———————————————— Date ————————————————

INTRODUCTORY NARRATIVE

Read the following narrative to discover how a camera club activity taught Erin about producing an oral presentation.

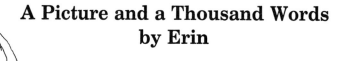

A Picture and a Thousand Words
by Erin

I've been in the camera club for three years now, and I really enjoy it. I hope to be a professional photographer some day. My dream is to work for *National Geographic* and spend my life traveling to exotic places to photograph wildlife and natural settings. Much of my enthusiasm for photography comes from Mr. Martin, who is our club sponsor/adviser. He not only teaches us about equipment and techniques, but he also finds opportunities for us to display our photography and present our knowledge to others. Recently Mr. Martin organized a large photography display at a local shopping mall. As a part of the exhibit he asked the members of the club to make presentations about various aspects of photography (history, famous photographers, camera equipment, terminology, and so forth). Each of us had to produce an oral presentation about a specific topic and present it several times over a three-day weekend.

The presentations went very smoothly and we received numerous compliments on the quality of our "lectures." There is a reason for that: Mr. Martin had us well prepared. He gave us some reading material that explained how to make an oral presentation, and we used this as a basis for discussions about preparing for the "big event." He also gave us plenty of time (while sternly warning us about procrastination) and help with such things as developing visual aids, locating factual information, organizing exhibit displays, and practicing presentation skills. We made dress rehearsal presentations at our last club meeting and offered one another constructive criticism, which focused each of us on specific areas that were strong or that needed improvement. When the first day of the mall show arrived, everyone felt confident and ready to do his or her best.

As we worked on our projects and discussed the mechanics and components of a good oral presentation, I realized that we were learning things that go beyond photography. When I mentioned this to Mr. Martin, he smiled and nodded in agreement. He is, he said, a teacher first, and then a photographer. The experience of making oral presentations was not designed to make us better photographers, but to help us learn some important communication skills. He said that in the future most of us will have a need for these skills and be glad to have them. I think he's right.

© 1990 by The Center for Applied Research in Education

Name _____ Date _____

READING MATERIAL

Erin's camera club spent several weeks getting ready for the photography exhibit at the mall. To start out, Mr. Martin gave the students an information sheet which summarized what a person must do to prepare to make an oral presentation. Using this as a basis for discussion, Mr. Martin led them through a detailed examination of the skills one must acquire and the steps one must take to produce a quality oral presentation. You can benefit from the same advice; below is a copy of the information sheet Mr. Martin gave the club members. Read it carefully before beginning the Classroom Assignment.

Confidence, Preparedness, and Style:
Three Elements of a Successful Oral Presentation

One of the most important keys to making an effective oral presentation is to speak to the audience in a way that makes them feel comfortable and ready to listen. The ability to do this centers on three interconnected areas: confidence, preparedness, and style. Let's look at each area separately to identify what you should consider when preparing an oral presentation.

Confidence

Confidence comes with experience. The more oral presentations you give, the more comfortable you will be giving them. That's why practice counts. Practicing before friends, family, or even a mirror will increase your self-assurance. Confidence also comes from understanding what has to be done, believing that you can do it, and knowing that you are prepared on the day of your presentation.

Preparation Equals Preparedness

The key ingredients of preparation are: (1) adequate research, with accurate data collection; (2) logical organization; (3) informative visual aids; (4) a thorough knowledge of the subject; (5) plenty of practice; (6) a written "script" (a paper, outline, or collection of notecards); and (7) confidence in your ability to do a good job.

Research is usually best done in a library or resource center. Record your facts on notecards, because they can be arranged and rearranged on a desktop when it is time to start organizing the presentation. A bibliography of sources should also be kept. After you have arranged the notecards into groups and subgroups, use that arrangement to make a detailed outline, which will serve as a model for the presentation. Next, write the full-length text of the talk out in paragraph form, even if you plan to speak only from notes, because writing it out helps develop and organize each point in your presentation.

To design visual aids, consult your outline for those points that may need additional emphasis and clarification or that may be of particular interest to the audience. You may want to use posters, models, dioramas, charts, graphs, diagrams, slides, videotape, demonstrations, or exhibits.

READING MATERIAL, CONT'D

Take advantage of all the time you have available to prepare: preparedness comes from steady, concentrated effort, not a last minute scramble.

Style

Keep your audience in mind as you write the material for an oral presentation, because if you write a boring report, you will certainly make a boring presentation. If possible, include humor, because a smiling audience is a receptive audience. Present information in terms your audience can understand. Be concise—state points completely but as briefly as possible. Concentrate on continuity—help the audience follow your thoughts by giving them a presentation that flows from one idea or fact to the next. Include references to visual materials and specify certain places in the presentation where you will explain your visual aids to the audience. Always ask if there are any questions when you finish a presentation; this is an important courtesy and also demonstrates your confidence in your knowledge of the topic.

There are also many physical aspects to style. Pay attention to your body language—how you stand, hold your shoulders, move your hands, and dress all give the audience an impression of you. Try to avoid nervous habits like twirling your hair, drumming your fingers or rocking back and forth on your heels. It helps to make eye contact, to project your voice, use English properly, vary your inflection (have you ever had to listen to a long lecture given in a monotone?), articulate words clearly, and be enthusiastic. A stylish speaker is aware of all these things but does not overdo any of them. Again, practice makes all the difference. If you can walk up to give your presentation confident in your own preparation, including practice in the matters of style, you can't help but give a good presentation.

Name _____ Date _____

CLASSROOM ASSIGNMENT

Working individually or in a small group (your teacher will decide which), choose *one* of the assignments below to complete by the end of the next class period. A rough draft should be started today, and a final draft should be ready to hand in by the end of the period tomorrow. You may also be asked to present your work to the class for discussion.

Assume you are preparing materials for a junior high (or middle) school English class that is learning about making oral presentations. Your assignment is to develop a handout or information sheet that can be used to help teach the class. Choose *one* assignment below, and do your best to produce a clear, straightforward document that would help a seventh or eighth grade student better understand what is required to prepare for and present an oral report.

Assignment 1: Develop an "Oral Presentation Evaluation Sheet," itemizing specific points that a teacher would evaluate during an oral presentation. Give each item a point value to indicate how much weight it has in the overall evaluation, and make the total evaluation worth 100 points.

Assignment 2: Develop a checklist that students can use to determine if they are ready to give an oral presentation. Include everything you can think of that a student should have done to prepare for such a project. Write each item as a question that can be answered "yes" or "no," and be as specific as possible. An example item might be: "Can I pronounce all the words in my report?" The checklist should be designed for students to use about a week before presentations are to be given so that deficiencies and problems can be taken care of.

Assignment 3: Develop a list of suggestions and advice for students who are about to begin a project that will require oral presentations. What will you tell them to do to help ensure a quality project? How should they get started? What roadblocks might they encounter? Your list may include skills they will need, the order in which they should do things, ideas for conducting research, and suggestions for preparing to give an oral presentation. Be as specific as possible; no detail is too trivial if it will give students an insight into the process of organizing and presenting an oral report.

Name _____ Date _____

ON YOUR OWN

Giving oral presentations is an important and valuable experience for high school students. For this lesson you will choose a topic from a subject area assigned by your teacher and prepare an oral presentation to be given in class. One presentation will be made per day over a period of five to six weeks, with each lasting no more than ten minutes. You will be given a due date, and on that day it will be your responsibilty to teach the class about the topic you have chosen.

Obviously the person who makes the first presentation will have less time to prepare than the last presenter (by as much as six weeks). For this reason, the order of presentation will be determined by drawing names from a hat. There will be two drawings: the first will be volunteers only and the second will be everyone who didn't volunteer to go first. To encourage people to volunteer (and to make the evaluation system more fair for the early presenters) a bonus of five points will be given to the first five people drawn. These people will have less preparation time and will also serve as models for later presentations. The bonus points are their reward for leading the way.

To complete this project, follow the assignment below:

    I. Record the subject area assigned by your teacher here: _____

_____

   II. Record your topic choice here: _____

_____

  III. Prepare an oral presentation about your topic. Your goal is to *teach* the class; to inform your fellow students about things you have learned through research and study. The presentation should be five to seven minutes long.

  IV. Design and produce a visual aid (such as a poster) to go along with your oral presentation.

   V. Be ready to give your presentation on this date: _____ .

  VI. Do not begin work on the presentation until you have received teacher approval of the topic recorded above.

        _____ Topic is approved

        _____ Choose a new topic

        Comments: _____

_____

_____

_____

 VII. Following the presentation there will be a brief question-answer period during which you are expected to answer reasonable questions from the class and from the teacher.

ACTIVITY 22.
Studying Current Issues

TEACHER PREVIEW

LESSON DESCRIPTIONS

Introductory Narrative ("As the World Turns"): John explains how a current events project in his history class helped him realize the importance of understanding the events of the modern world. He also tells about his teacher's approach to presenting current events in the classroom.

Reading Material: An article about teaching current events in secondary schools, written by John's teacher (Mrs. Blackwell), that she used as a reading assignment with her classes.

Classroom Assignment: PREPARATION REQUIRED. This is a three-class period lesson; an ample supply of recent newspapers and news magazines must be on hand at the beginning of the first period. Here is a synopsis of the project:

Day 1: Each student makes a list of issues or topics that are currently in the news, using newspapers and magazines as references. Then, in a discussion, students develop a composite class list of current events topics. Use your judgment at this point to eliminate any topics that would not be appropriate for a research project.

Day 2: Students are placed in small groups of two or three (possibly four), and each group chooses a topic from the list. The period is spent hunting for headlines, articles, photographs, captions, cartoons, editorials, and so forth that are related to the chosen topic. These materials are clipped and trimmed (scissors must be available), and the date and name of publication are written on each item. At the end of the period, each group puts its material in an envelope or a folder and turns it in.

Day 3: There are two assignments for this period, and you must decide which one to make. Each group is told to make either a scrapbook or a collage. You may assign all groups to do one or the other, or you may give the groups their choice. In either case, materials must be available: large format paper (for example, 12 × 18 manila or art paper) for the scrapbooks, and posterboard for collages. Also needed will be paste, glue, rubber cement, or tape for fastening clippings on paper or posterboard, and markers for making headings, titles, and covers.

On Your Own: Each student chooses a topic from the list developed during the Classroom Assignment and begins to follow it closely by reading, watching the news, and taking notes. Once a week the student writes a summary of the week's events in a journal. Journal entries are to be in complete sentences and proper paragraphs, but the style is to be informal, like diary entries or letters to friends. Opinions are encouraged, but the distinction between opinions and facts must be clearly made.

At the outset of the project you must decide how long it will last and how often journals will be collected and inspected (or graded). Specific dates should be determined because the individual assignment sheet has spaces for them to be recorded. The length of the project can be anything from four weeks to a full semester. The assignment sheet has an evaluation chart for the mid-project inspections, so students should be instructed to hand in the sheets with their journals. The finished journals can be given a letter grade, based upon whatever criteria you wish to establish.

SUGGESTIONS FOR SETTING THE STAGE

- Bring a video tape of an evening news broadcast and show it to the class. Use it to initiate discussion about specific topics that are being reported. Also, count the number of stories that are presented in a half hour newscast, to illustrate how much is taking place each day.

- Prepare a current events quiz to give your class. Watch the news and read newspapers and magazines for a week, while keeping a notebook in which multiple choice, fill-in-the-blank, true-false, and matching questions can be recorded. Don't invent trick questions; keep everything straightforward and simple. After giving the quiz, go over the answers and discuss why students should know about these things.

- Give each student an outline desk map of the world (one that does not have places labeled), then read them a series of news briefs that mention places in the world. For example, you might say, "Terrorists hijacked a passenger jet this afternoon and forced it to fly to the island of Cyprus, where it landed and is now sitting on a runway at the airport in the capital city of Nicosia." After reading this, show students where Cyprus is, on a wall map, and instruct them to locate Cyprus on their maps, circle it, and label it #1. Then read a second bulletin, perhaps about South Africa, or Ireland, or Australia. Do about fifteen or twenty of these, and then discuss the importance of knowing geography to understand current events. Don't make up the events you are reporting; use real items from the recent news for this activity.

Name _____ Date _____

INTRODUCTORY NARRATIVE

Read the following narrative to learn how John became interested in studying and understanding current events.

As the World Turns
by John

Until recently I lived in a self-made cocoon, surrounded by all the familiar things that made it seem like the world would never change. It was a comfortable feeling of well-being, everything was predictable and I was serenely unaware of anything happening beyond the friendly confines of my family, my school, and my community. But as I grew older I began to be vaguely aware that major events were occurring in the country and around the world. I didn't understand them, so I tried to ignore them, in the belief that they had little relevance to my life. This year, however, I have been influenced by a teacher who believes that every person has an *obligation* to know what's going on in the world. She has opened my eyes to the need to be an informed person.

Mrs. Blackwell takes the study of current events seriously. She says that it is the perfect way to integrate history with geography and sociology, while at the same time introducing students to the world in which they live. In her history class we talk about current events at least twice a week. She has the amazing ability to link virtually any current event to something that has happened in history. Discussions of current events always seem to lead right into a history lesson, and the lesson helps explain why certain things are happening today. I like studying history this way. It makes what I learn more meaningful.

To get us started on the study of current events, Mrs. Blackwell gave us copies of a magazine article she wrote two years ago, "The Importance of Current Events in the Secondary Curriculum." It was published for teachers, but she intentionally wrote it so that high school students could benefit from it, too. After reading and analyzing the article, we spent the first semester discussing a wide range of topics that appeared in the news. This was our introduction to current events, and it was very effective in opening our eyes to the world around us.

Now as we enter the second semester we are beginning a new current events project. Each student has chosen an issue, topic, or concern and is studying it closely for the entire semester. We are expected to make notes as we watch the news, read newspapers, and carefully examine at least one news magazine each week to become as informed about our topics as possible. Our assignment is to keep a "Current Events Journal" that summarizes what has happened during each week of the semester. Entries must be dated for the Friday or Saturday of the week, and they are to be written in a narrative style, almost like writing in a diary. On the first Monday of the month Mrs. Blackwell will collect the journals, grade them, and return them before Friday, when the next entries are due.

I am enjoying this assignment, even though I don't understand everything that's going on. My topic is the Middle East; specifically, relations between Israel and the surrounding Arab nations (as well as the Palestinians). I've already learned a lot even though the project has just begun. I intend to work hard on this assignment, because I agree with Mrs. Blackwell. The entire world is now our community, and it is absolutely vital that we become informed citizens.

Name ⎯⎯⎯⎯⎯⎯⎯⎯⎯⎯⎯⎯⎯⎯ Date ⎯⎯⎯⎯⎯⎯⎯⎯⎯⎯⎯⎯

READING MATERIAL

Read the following article to see how Mrs. Blackwell explains the value of current events for high school students. As you read, see if you agree with the points she makes.

The Importance of Current Events
in the Secondary Curriculum
by Mary Beth Blackwell

I began teaching current events in the early 1970s. We were in the midst of Watergate, and the Vietnam War had divided the country. My students were barraged with news about scandals, plots, casualties, protests, dirty tricks, POWs, inflation, lost prestige, an Arab Oil embargo, Communist aggression, pollution, and innumerable other issues. They had a keen awareness that many important things were going on, but what they saw and heard every day seemed complicated and confusing. I told them that studying current events is like following a soap opera: when you first watch you have no idea who the characters are, how they relate to one another, or really what's going on at all. But by tuning in regularly the plot soon becomes much clearer because you have a background of knowledge. Gradually it seems less a mystery and more a continuing drama. And so it is with current events: the longer you watch, the more comprehensible the story becomes.

I believe that it is absolutely essential to teach our students about the world of today. Their future problems are incubating right now. It is obviously easier to understand a problem if its origins can be traced, and the origins of the political, social, economic, environmental, and international problems of tomorrow will be in the news tonight.

Current events study opens students' eyes to the world about them. It allows them to watch what's happening and therefore begin to understand the forces that shape history. Most traditional curricula systematically exclude a vast number of timely and very important topics simply because they are too recent (or too diverse) to include in textbooks. Current events allow teachers to update social studies books and to teach history as a series of events which have caused the present to be as it is. Courses in current events help students to understand that they are in the midst of a huge ongoing story and that the "news" is feeding them valuable information one day at a time. Once students recognize this, they understand that in the future they will *know* the history of the recent past because they studied it while it happened. Then the events of the world will be comprehensible, if not sensible. In the final analysis, the payoff for teaching current events is that people trained to watch, study, and understand current events make intelligent voters and informed leaders, and they help create strong communities.

One note: It is fairly common for students to have nightmares about atomic bombs, terrorized people, foreign wars, drug trafficking, AIDS, pollution, unemployed parents, and so forth, if that is the spectre raised in the classroom. Out of terror a horse will run back into a burning barn. The fear is warranted, but the response is completely wrong. I tell my students they *should* fear atomic war, a polluted environment, and all the rest, but the proper response is to watch what is happening, gain a thorough understanding, and find solutions to the problems. If students see that problems can be coped with, their fear will stem from respectful understanding of danger, not blind terror.

READING MATERIAL, CONT'D

I can't help thinking about the leaders of the twenty-first century. They are sitting in classrooms all across America right now. They need training that cannot be included in textbooks. They simply *must* have the ability to follow current events and create or think of solutions to problems as they arise. We need to challenge tomorrow's leaders by directing their creative thinking toward important, meaningful issues. And if the nations of the world are going to peacefully coexist, then the children of the world must be taught about one another and the things that link their countries together. A perfect example is a student I once had. He was enthralled by "super heroes" when he came into my class in September. Although extremely intelligent, he had little knowledge of what was going on in the world, and he poured hundreds of hours into reading comic books and creating his own super-hero characters. He took his hobby very seriously until he began investigating current events. At some point he decided that studying the Middle East was more important than composing super-hero stories, and he became our resident authority on Middle East affairs. He found that he had family ties in Lebanon, and he began to conduct independent research. In short, he turned current events into his personal hobby. His expertise may prove invaluable in the next century. This, to me, is the ultimate reward of teaching current events.

Name _____ **Date** _____

CLASSROOM ASSIGNMENT

© 1990 by The Center for Applied Research in Education

DAY 1

Begin this lesson by making a list of issues or topics that are currently in the news. There are newspapers and news magazines in the room to help you develop a list. Be ready to share your list with the class in a discussion during the last part of the period. A composite list of current events topics will be recorded for use in tomorrow's class.

DAY 2

For this project you will work in a small group of two, three, or four students. As a group, choose one of the topics from the list and search through magazines and newspapers to find information about it. Clip the headlines, articles, cartoons, editorials, and so forth that you find and trim them neatly. Take time to read them over so you know what they are about, then file them in a folder or envelope which you will be given. Be careful when clipping articles so as not to destroy material that may be useful to other groups, and be sure to put a date and name of source on each clipping. Continue collecting material until the end of the period, and then hand your group's clippings in.

DAY 3

Your teacher will assign *one* of these two activities for your group to work on:

1. Make a current events scrapbook by arranging your clippings on pages that will be bound together. Leave at least one inch for a left hand margin so that the pages can be stapled. The organization of the scrapbook is left up to you. Make a cover for the scrapbook that clearly tells what topic your group investigated.

2. Make a current events collage by arranging your clippings on a piece of posterboard. The layout of the collage is left up to you, except that it must have a heading that clearly tells what topic your group investigated.

Name _____   Date _____

ON YOUR OWN

Choose a current event from the list made in class. You will be following this topic for a period of time, so be careful to select something you find interesting. As soon as you have decided on a topic, begin studying it by reading newspapers and magazines and by watching television news programs. Record your topic here:

_____

Now follow this assignment:

   I. Keep a journal about the issue, topic, or area of concern that you have chosen to study. The journal should be written on $8\frac{1}{2}'' \times 11''$ white lined composition paper unless otherwise instructed. Write in complete sentences and proper paragraphs and use your best handwriting.

  II. Make one entry in the journal each week summarizing the things that have happened over the past seven days. These entries should be written informally, like entries in a diary or letters to a friend. You may include your opinions, but be sure to make clear distinctions between fact and opinion.

 III. The duration of this project will be determined by your teacher.

The project begins on this date: _____

The project ends on this date: _____

 IV. Journals will be inspected periodically during this project. You are expected to have your journal in class, ready to hand in for inspection, on these dates:

Due Date	Excellent	Satisfactory	Needs Work	Incomplete
1. _____	_____	_____	_____	_____
2. _____	_____	_____	_____	_____
3. _____	_____	_____	_____	_____
4. _____	_____	_____	_____	_____
5. _____	_____	_____	_____	_____

Final Grade _____

COMMENTS:

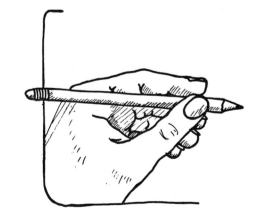

ACTIVITY 23.
Writing About Your World

TEACHER PREVIEW

LESSON DESCRIPTIONS

Introductory Narrative ("For Future Reference"): Jason tells about his discovery of an old newspaper and how he used it as a reference for a research project. He also describes an activity his teacher designed, based on his idea of writing a current events paper for someone in the future to read.

Reading Material: Jason's paper about the events of one day: December 23, 1968, written as if seen through the eyes of a seventeen-year-old high school student who is reading the morning newspaper.

Classroom Assignment: PREPARATION REQUIRED. Students imagine that they are journalists in the year 2025, preparing to write articles about events from the final decade of the twentieth century that have had an effect on the first quarter of the twenty-first century. Their primary resources are newspapers and news magazines from the period. When an appropriate article is located, a student fills out a "Preliminary Research Data Sheet" on which he or she records the main ideas of the article, explains why the article is of interest to people in the year 2025, and offers some opinions about the event. Students look through magazines and newspapers for articles and choose the number that you assign (between one and three). A "Data Sheet" (provided with the "Classroom Assignment") is filled out for each selected article, and the completed Data Sheets are turned in at the end of the period. Newspapers (or news magazines) must be on hand for this assignment. Also, the assignment may be extended to two or more class periods if you feel this would be beneficial.

On Your Own: Each student writes an essay about the present that would help describe the 1990s to a person in the year 2025. The assignment sheet provides a list of thirty current event subject areas, and each student must choose at least three of these areas to emphasize in the essay. After the essays are graded and returned, students put their writings in "time capsules," which are 9″ × 12″ envelopes. They are encouraged to include additional writings, clippings, and other mementos of the 1990s in their envelopes before sealing them. The envelopes are labeled as time capsules to be opened in the year 2025, and students are told to put them in attics or with other personal belongings that are being saved.

SUGGESTIONS FOR SETTING THE STAGE

- Have a class discussion about events that are happening right now that will affect the future. Develop a list on the board and ask students to make some predictions about where these events may be leading. Is the class generally optimistic or pessimistic about the future? Do the students think that people in the year 2025 will look favorably upon the way things were handled in the 1990s? What things might they criticize and what things might they praise?

- Tell your students that each has the miraculous power to eliminate *one* problem from the face of the Earth. What would it be? Have them write their answers down, along with good reasons, and be prepared to share and defend them with the class. Each student should be able to justify his or her decision to someone who chose a different problem. In other words, why was one problem chosen over another? Instruct them to avoid general answers like "war," and "disease." Instead, they should be very specific; for example: "I would put an end to the trouble between Palestinians and Israelis," or "I would destroy the AIDS virus," or "I would vaporize all ICBMs." Use the answers students give as a basis for discussing the problems facing the modern world as we approach the twenty-first century.

- Place students in groups of three to four. Give the groups a limited amount of time (up to fifteen minutes) to list as many current events as possible. These should be things that have occurred in the last year or so. When time is up, each group turns in its list for evaluation. This activity will give you a handle on the level of awareness your students have of current events. This should lead to discussions, activities, or lessons that will help fill in gaps in your students' knowledge or take advantage of their areas of interest.

Name _____   Date _____

INTRODUCTORY NARRATIVE

Read the following narrative for an explanation of Jason's interest in writing about the present as a way of communicating with the future.

For Future Reference
by Jason

Last summer my parents rented a house on a beautiful lake in Michigan for a three-week vacation. We had a lot of fun there, and it was a great vacation. One day my dad, my sister, and I wanted to go fishing, but we only had two poles. The landlord said there might be some in the attic, so I climbed up to see. Sure enough, there were some fishing poles next to a pile of old newspapers. As I gathered up the poles, the headline on the top paper caught my attention: "Apollo 8 Still On Course: Moon Orbit is Christmas Eve Target." "Wow," I thought, "Now *there's* some history!" I picked up the paper and took it downstairs with me. That night before going to sleep I read through it. Reading a newspaper from 1968 was like opening a time capsule and having history come alive. It was a fascinating experience, and it led to a truly unique project when I came back to school this fall.

I am enrolled in Mr. Vandenberg's course, "Modern America," which focuses on American history and society since the end of World War II. One of our first assignments was a research project. Each of us had to choose a topic (from a list developed during class) and write a brief explanation or description of it. These papers were read to the class and became the basis of discussions for a two-week period. I asked for permission to write about a specific day, December 23, 1968), as seen through the eyes of a seventeen-year old high school student who is reading the morning newspaper. Mr. Vandenberg liked the idea very much, and so my discovery in the attic of our vacation house led to a history class research activity.

But my idea became more than just a personal project. When Mr. Vandenberg read my paper it impressed him enough to incorporate the idea into his curriculum. We are now preparing to write our own papers based on the current events of today. These, along with anything else we wish to include, will be placed in envelopes (or boxes) and sealed. Instructions written in indelible ink on the outside will tell someone from the next generation not to open the "time capsule" until the year 2025. At the quarter mark of the twenty-first century it should be interesting to read a report from a high school student who was watching not only a century but a millennium begin to change. I like the assignment, not just because I helped think of it, but because I can imagine my own offspring reading what I've written. I guess it's like studying my roots in reverse: I'm providing something that will help my children get to know me better.

Name _____ Date _____

READING MATERIAL

Reading about past events, as seen through the eyes of someone who lived at the time, is an interesting way to learn about history. Many of our best and most informative historical records are the personal letters, journals, and diaries of people who wrote about events great and small as they occurred. Below is the paper Jason wrote about events in December, 1968. He based his report on a newspaper that he found, and he wrote in first person, present tense, as if he were a high school student reading the newspaper during Christmas vacation, 1968. He tells what the main stories in that evening's newspaper were and gives his impressions of some of the issues.

Read Jason's paper below, and think about how you would compose such a document for your world today. What style of writing would you use and what kinds of information would you include? Also see if any of the events Jason mentions are familiar to you. They were major stories in 1968, and many of them have important historical significance.

A Day in the Life
by Jason Birdwell

My title is borrowed from last year's popular Beatles album, "Sgt. Pepper's Lonely Hearts Club Band." I'm writing about the events of one day in my life, December 23, 1968, as they were reported in this morning's newspaper. I hope this report will make interesting reading for someone in the future.

At 3:29 p.m. today the Apollo 8 spacecraft will be 202,700 miles from Earth and 34,500 miles from the moon. This is the exact point where the moon's gravity will be stronger than the Earth's. These are the first humans to have been in the gravitational grasp of anything but their own planet. The astronauts are Frank Borman, James A. Lovell Jr., and William Anders. There is a picture of Major Anders floating in the spacecraft, holding a camera lens. It is really amazing to see men floating in space, headed for the moon. I can remember when President Kennedy made a speech saying that we would land a man on the moon by the end of the decade. Although these astronauts will not land, they will orbit for 20 hours before returning home. It looks like President Kennedy's dream will be fulfilled. There should be a manned lunar landing in 1969.

The Apollo 8 mission was almost shortened due to sickness. All three astronauts had the 24-hour flu, with Frank Borman being the sickest. Today they are all feeling better, and the mission will continue as scheduled. When the spacecraft disappears behind the moon on its first approach, it will make a critical engine burn that will propel it into moon orbit. We will be out of touch with Apollo 8 for several minutes while it's behind the moon, so we won't know if the engines fired properly until it reappears. Those will be a tense few moments, but I am certain that everything will go smoothly. This event, man's first venture to the moon, is undoubtedly historic. It is exciting to live in such times.

There are other events in today's paper worth mentioning. After eleven months in captivity, the surviving eighty-two crewmen of the U.S. intelligence (spy) ship Pueblo were freed today by North Korea. According to the U.S. government, the North Koreans illegally seized the unarmed ship (which was filled with electronic detection equipment) outside their territorial waters, but North Korea said the crew had broken international law. Commander

READING MATERIAL, CONT'D

Lloyd M. Bucher said he and his men were beaten just last week, leaving some in "very bad physical condition." After hospital treatment in Seoul, South Korea, the crew will be returned home to their happy and relieved families.

In Vietnam, the Communists launched a series of heavy attacks across South Vietnam. The heaviest fighting, often at hand-to-hand range, saw mortars and rockets falling on American troops at the rate of 100 per minute. A force of 1,500 freshly equipped North Vietnamese swept out of Cambodia yesterday morning and lost at least 103 dead in a six-hour attack on an American patrol base 44 miles northwest of Saigon. The U.S. infantrymen, in deep bunkers but outnumbered by three-to-one, reported seventeen of their men killed and twelve wounded. The North Vietnamese blasted their way through barbed wire with bazookas and fought in the trenches connecting the bunkers. At least thirty enemy bodies were left strung alone the barbed wire.

Meanwhile, South Vietnamese Vice President Nguyen Cao Ky boarded a plane in Paris and headed back to Saigon to report to his government on the Paris peace talks. Apparently Secretary of Defense Clark Clifford is putting a lot of pressure on him to stop stalling with ridiculous arguments about what shape the negotiation table should be, and get started on a peace plan. President-elect Nixon wants to shift the fighting in Vietnam to Vietnamese troops and gradually withdraw American troops. The South Vietnamese government doesn't want this to happen, and it is "brickwalling" the peace talks. We can count on continuing the war in 1969. More than 30,000 Americans have died in Vietnam since December 22, 1961. Almost half of the death toll has occurred this year: between January 1, 1968 and last week, 14,038 servicemen died in Vietnam.

Today the U.S. president is Lyndon B. Johnson, but on January 20 our new president, Richard M. Nixon, will take office. Yesterday Mr. Nixon attended the wedding and reception of his daughter, Julie, and her new husband, Dwight David Eisenhower II (President Eisenhower's grandson). Following the reception, Mr. Nixon said he is heading for Florida to relax in the sun for a few days before making final preparations to become President of the United States.

Here are a few additional items that may be of interest: The country is in the midst of a "Hong Kong flu" epidemic; perhaps 30 million people will get it. Fidel Castro begins his second decade as communist leader of Cuba; he came to power on January 1, 1959. Signs of runaway inflation are beginning to show all through the economy. The International Longshoremen's Association is on strike, which has tied up ports from Maine to Texas. Without explanation, Equatorial Guinea (in West Africa) ordered a halt to a Red Cross airlift of food and supplies to starving people in Biafra, where over 850,000 people are suffering from famine; most of these people are children. One of the oldest cities in North America, Saulte Ste. Marie, Michigan, celebrates its 300th birthday this year. U.C.L.A. once again has the best college basketball team in the country, and it seems likely to continue having the top team for years to come. President Johnson will send his final economic message to Congress in the next week or two, and he's expected to focus on balancing the trade deficit. Finally, the price of food: today's paper advertises ham, 79¢ a pound; soda pop, $1 for twelve cans; salad dressing, 35¢ for one quart; cream cheese, 29¢ for 8 oz.; flour, $1.89 for 25 pounds; macintosh apples, 39¢ for 3 pounds; yellow onions, 39¢ for 3 pounds; and brown and serve rolls, 29¢ for one dozen.

The paper also lists the five most important events of 1968, which I'd like to include:

1. Robert F. Kennedy was shot and critically wounded in a Los Angeles hotel after winning the California primary on June 5; he died on June 6.

2. Martin Luther King, Jr. was shot and killed outside his Memphis motel room on April 4.

READING MATERIAL, CONT'D

3. On January 23, North Korea seized the U.S. Navy ship *Pueblo* and took eighty-three prisoners.

4. On March 31, President Johnson announced that he would not seek reelection.

5. On August 20, Soviet Union and Warsaw Pact forces invaded Czechoslovakia to crush a liberal regime.

Well, those are the main stories. I think they are all important, to me personally, and historically as well. I'm 17, and the war in Vietnam is looming ever larger. It's something that dominates conversations these days. The election of Mr. Nixon could have a major impact on my life, depending on how he decides to handle the war. I hope he's a good president. The Pueblo incident has been a major item in the news for months, and of course, the Apollo flight is the beginning of a new era, the space age. By the time I'm fifty we'll probably have space stations and moon colonies and maybe even an outpost on mars. I guess the old saying "The sky's the limit" no longer applies. We've gone beyond the sky and I doubt if we'll ever come back.

Name _____ Date _____

CLASSROOM ASSIGNMENT

Imagine that you are a journalist, in the year 2025, preparing to write an article about the history of the world during the final decade of the twentieth century. Using microfilm copies of daily newspapers and weekly news magazines from the 1990s, you scan material for stories that are connected in some way to events in 2025. When one is located, you list its main ideas and record your thoughts about why the article might be useful, along with your own opinions about it. You also note where the information came from so it can be easily located for further research later.

Fill out the Preliminary Research Data Sheet as if you were preparing such a piece. Your teacher will tell you how many articles to study for this assignment; fill out one Data Sheet for each article you read. Remember to write in the voice of a journalist/researcher from the year 2025. There are places on the Data Sheet where you can record your own thoughts, opinions, and comments, so use your imagination, be creative, and project your mind to that future time. How will the next generation view the things that are going on in the world right now?

Name _____   Date _____

PRELIMINARY RESEARCH DATA SHEET

Property of _____

Begun on this date: _____ 2025 A.D.

Name of publication: _____

Date of issue: _____

Article no. _____ Headline _____

Page _____

Three main ideas from the article:

1.

2.

3.

Explain why this article is of interest to the current world of 2025 (use a separate piece of paper if more space is needed):

In your opinion, did the event or issue described in this article reveal a positive or a negative direction for humanity? Explain your answer (use a separate piece of paper if more space is needed):

Name _____   Date _____

ON YOUR OWN

Write an essay about the present world that would help describe the 1990s to a person in the year 2025. Include information from at least three of the areas listed below, but don't develop a research paper: this essay should explain what's going on, but also (and more important) it should record your opinions and feelings about the events and issues of your world.

Record three areas of current events from the list below about which you intend to write:

1. _____

2. _____

3. _____

National wars	The arms race	China
Civil wars	The space program	Africa
Technology	Fads	South America
Transportation	Health	Central America
Communication	Science	Japan
Religion	Natural disasters	Medicine
Politics	Manmade disasters	Fashion
World leaders	The Middle East	Education
The economy	Europe	Poverty/unemployment
Environmental concerns	The U.S.S.R.	Sports

Your essay may be written in any form you wish: as a letter, an editorial, a diary entry, or a simple essay. Your essay is due on: _____ .

When the graded essay is returned, it will be sealed in an envelope (along with clippings and any other personal papers you wish to include) to be stored in an attic or with other "memorabilia" that you intend to keep. The envelope will be labeled: "Please Open in 2025." It is a mini-record of what life was like in the 1990s, and it will be very interesting for you or someone else to read years from now.

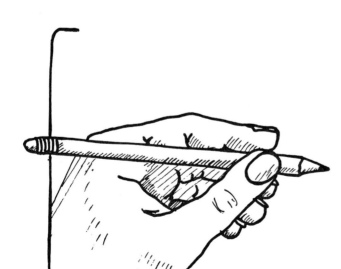

ACTIVITY 24.
Learning to Learn

TEACHER PREVIEW

LESSON DESCRIPTIONS

Introductory Narrative ("Digging Deeper"): Amanda explains how she became interested in whales and marine biology following a brief discussion in her biology class.

Reading Material: A paper that Amanda wrote for her English class about becoming a marine biologist and studying whales.

Classroom Assignment: Students write about what career they would choose if they had to make a decision today. They focus on what factors in their lives have influenced them to make their career choices. Emphasis is placed on extending the simple lessons of daily life into major decisions and career goals.

On Your Own: Students write essays designed to be endorsements of specific jobs or occupational fields.

SUGGESTIONS FOR SETTING THE STAGE

- Initiate a discussion about the many interests of high school students that are never studied or even discussed in most classes. Then talk about individual interests within the class and ask your students to explain how they became interested in these things. Point out that quite often all it takes is a brief introduction to a subject to become fascinated with it, which leads to a desire to learn more. Impress upon your students that learning about topics that interest them can be a very rewarding experience.

- Bring pictures of whales (or other oceanography topics) to class, and ask your students if they have ever thought of studying them. Discuss their importance: their place in the ecosystem of the sea and their beauty. Focus your students' attention on the wide variety of topics oceanography offers for study, and suggest that it is typical of many other areas that high school students usually don't think of when contemplating their future occupations. Encourage your students to look into areas of interest and search out potential careers.

- In a class discussion about the modern world, ask students to think of things that probably will be different ten or twenty years from now. Explain that in a rapidly changing world, success is dependent upon adaptability and independent learning. Learning on your own will be an important skill in the twenty-first century.

Name _____ Date _____

INTRODUCTORY NARRATIVE

Read the following narrative to find out how Amanda transformed a twenty-minute lesson on whales into an independent study project and then into a career goal.

Digging Deeper
by Amanda

I don't think Mrs. Larson even knows she had an impact on my life; I've never told her. I liked her as a biology teacher, and I learned a great deal from her. She had the creative energy that all good teachers have. But her real influence in my life can be traced to a mere twenty-minute period of time taken from a Friday afternoon class last October. She came into the biology lab and said:

Today I want to spend a few minutes introducing you to my favorite subject, the study of whales. Since I was a girl I've wanted to know about them. To me, they're one of the highest and most exquisite forms of life on earth. To know about whales is to know about the grandest animal of them all. Listen carefully as I read one paragraph from Herman Melville's *Moby Dick.* See if you can decipher his message about life in general as he describes his efforts to write about whales.

'One often hears of writers that rise and swell with their subject, though it may seem but an ordinary one. How, then, with me, writing of this Leviathan? Unconsciously my chirography expands into placard capitals. Give me a condor's quill! Give me Vesuvius' crater for an inkstand! Friends, hold my arms! For in the mere act of penning my thoughts of Leviathan, they weary me, and make me faint with their outstretching comprehensiveness of sweep, as if to include the whole circle of the sciences, and all the generations of whales, and men, and mastadons, past, present, and to come, with all the revolving panoramas of empire on earth, and throughout the whole universe, not excluding its suburbs. Such, and so magnifying, is the virtue of a large and liberal theme! We expand to its bulk. To produce a mighty book, you must choose a mighty theme. No great and enduring volume can ever be written on the flea, though many there be who have tried it.*

Mrs. Larson then continued,

Ladies and gentlemen, one piece of advice. Choose a mighty theme for your life and expand to its bulk. Don't limit yourselves to small, insignificant aspirations. Try to produce a mighty book. And may I suggest, for those who are so inclined, that the study of whales is a fine way to spend your life.

*Herman Melville, *Moby Dick*, The New American Library of World Literature, Inc., 1980, p. 432.

INTRODUCTORY NARRATIVE, CONT'D

That twenty minute discourse changed my life. It excited my curiosity about whales, which in turn (after extensive investigation) led to a career decision: I've decided to become a marine biologist.

The day following Mrs. Larson's lecture on whales, I went to the library in hot pursuit of more information about marine biology. I identified several colleges that offer marine biology programs, and I discovered that a good job is dependent upon an advanced degree, which requires courses in chemistry, physics, mathematics, botany, zoology, and other science areas. Undaunted, I began to investigate whales. The more I learned, the more fascinated I became with the subject. Until this time in my life I had never been truly motivated to learn all I could about something, but now I really wanted to *know* about life beneath the surface of the sea. I found books and articles about a wide variety of interesting topics. After nearly three hours in the library, I headed home with a stack of books in my arms. On top of the stack was a copy of *Moby Dick*.

Name _____ Date _____

READING MATERIAL

Today's world is complex and rapidly changing. Any serious observer of current events will tell you that modern technology and an ever-increasing volume of knowledge have combined to make it impossible to learn about *everything*. One must be selective. At the same time, through no fault of their own, schools have difficulty making time for the vast number of subjects that could potentially be taught in their classrooms. So what's a student who wants to learn about something that isn't offered in school to do? You can learn how to learn on your own.

The ultimate responsibility for preparing to live in a complicated world lies with the individual. Those who realize this truth will prosper in the new century. The essay below was written by Amanda for her English teacher in the spring of her senior year. The assignment was to write a persuasive endorsement of a job or occupational field. Each student wrote an essay that was designed to point out the benefits, highlights, and meaningfulness of a certain occupation. Amanda chose to write about studying whales as a marine biologist.

Marine Biology
by Amanda Covington

Whales are a mystery. They have survived humanity's attempt to exterminate them without giving up many of their secrets. Luckily, over the years a few dedicated people have decided that it is better to study than destroy them. These people are marine biologists. They are busy at work, trying to discover all they can about whales and how they fit into their ocean environment.

Imagine being under water in close proximity to a humpback whale. Hear it sing its song! See its huge dark form pass silently and effortlessly through the open sea! The magnificence of its presence is breathtaking. The beauty of its surroundings adds to the effect of an ethereal fantasy on a gigantic scale. But you are there! This is your job! The marine biologist goes to work each day by leaving the human world and entering the silent deep. One need not travel to outer space to find unexplored frontiers; the marine biologist finds them in his (or her) office, one hundred feet beneath any wave you choose. There the humpback, blue, and seventy-eight other species of whales live their lives.

Why should someone want to study whales? For one thing, they have been hunted almost to extinction, and it is worth any effort to save them. The blue whale was close to extinction in the late 1950s, and the numbers of sei, sperm, and fin whales were also drastically down. The world began to wake up to this tragedy, however, and in 1971 the United States declared commercially exploited whales to be endangered and prohibited the importation of all whale products. Of course, whales are still endangered since some countries have not banned whaling. 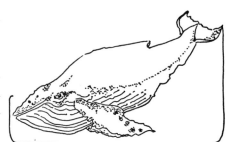 Marine biologists work to learn more about whales, to help protect them and also to satisfy their own unquenchable curiosities.

There is so much a person can learn about whales; even someone who is not a marine biologist can enjoy such a study. There are the toothed whales (odentoceti), which range in size from 4 feet to 60 feet, and the baleen whales (mysticeli) which range from 20 feet to 100 feet in length. The weight range of whales is 100 pounds to 150 tons. Some of the larger species can hold their breath for an hour or even longer. Mysticeli whales feed by straining large amounts

READING MATERIAL, CONT'D

of water through horny, fibrous mats of baleen that hang from the roof of the mouth. Odonticeti whales use teeth to seize prey, but the prey is not chewed, it is swallowed whole. The stomach is specially adapted to digest unchewed food. One of the most interesting facts about whales is that they exhibit epilemetic behavior. That is, one animal will help another animal when it is in trouble. Of course, the list of facts could continue, but the point is that whales are fascinating.

A marine biologist is a highly trained individual who has a specific interest in underwater life. Obviously, not all marine biologists study whales. There are many specialty areas within the field of marine biology. Some of these areas are just now emerging as technology allows us to dive deeper, stay under water longer, and analyze specimens more thoroughly. Underwater exploration and study is reserved for the adventurous and the curious, for those who want their life's work to be more exciting than their weekends and their vacations. This brief essay is an invitation to you, a future scientist, to consider the sea for your classroom and laboratory. You may find that it has an irresistible attraction for you. If so, you have the stuff of which marine biologists are made.

Name _____ Date _____

CLASSROOM ASSIGNMENT

Although many high school students do not make definite career decisions until after graduation, most juniors and seniors know where their interests lie. They have ideas of what they would *like* to do for their life's work. Where do these ideas come from? Why do some people become very interested in a certain occupation while others never even consider it as a possibility? Quite often adults play an important role in your choice of vocation. Through their work, their conversation and the things they accomplish, these people provide lessons about their specific careers. These lessons may be very brief, and the people providing them may be unaware that they are having an influence on you. For this reason, you have a special obligation to yourself to pursue the career lessons that come your way. In other words, you should extend the lessons and learn on your own so that you may take advantage of them.

This lesson asks you to identify and write about a person or event that influenced you to learn more, or think seriously, about an occupation. Follow the assignment below to complete the assignment.

If you had to choose a career for yourself today, what would it be? Who (or what) influenced you to choose this career? Your assignment is to write an essay describing how you became interested in a specific occupation area. As you write, answer these questions:

- What career would you choose if you had to make a decision today?
- When did you first become interested in this career?
- What *one* person or event sparked your interest in this career?
- *How* did the person or event influence your career decision? In other words, describe as clearly as possible the circumstances surrounding your decision.
- Since you first thought of this career as a possibility for your own life's work, what have you done to learn more about it?

Name _____ Date _____

ON YOUR OWN

"Learning on your own" is an idea that works in two directions. First, it means that it is possible to learn about specialized topics even if your teachers don't have time for them during class hours. Second, it means that others can be introduced to things that are of interest to *you*, thereby perhaps motivating someone else to learn about them independently. This assignment focuses on the second application.

Write an essay that is designed to point out the benefits, highlights, and meaningfulness of a certain occupation. The choice of occupation is left up to you. Compose the essay as if you were writing it to a younger student who is just beginning to think about career possibilities. Your paper should be an endorsement of a job or occupational field. Try to make the person to whom you are writing the essay believe that such a career is worth striving for. Give him or her good reasons for pursuing knowledge about the career through the coming years.

Your essay will require some research to make it authoritative and to ensure that it offers sound advice. Supply such information as the amount of education the job requires, special courses a student should take, the income level of people in the occupational field, local colleges that offer degrees that apply to the career area, and the kinds of work a person in this area actually performs.

Remember to be creative in your writing style and persuasive in your presentation of reasons for pursuing the career. The finished paper should be two to four pages long.

DUE DATE: _____

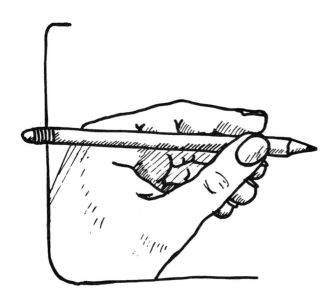

ACTIVITY 25.
Writing a Research Paper

TEACHER PREVIEW

LESSON DESCRIPTIONS

Introductory Narrative ("Just the Facts, Please"): Linda explains why she had to learn how to compose a research paper so she could write a report about primates in an effort to land a summer job at the city zoo. She also includes some advice she received from one of her teachers about how to approach a research/writing project.

Reading Material: A list of general considerations to keep in mind when preparing to write a research paper, followed by Linda's research paper about orang–utans.

Classroom Assignment: PREPARATION REQUIRED. Begin with a discussion of footnotes, using Linda's report as a model. Footnotes for periodicals should be specifically discussed since there are none in Linda's paper. Worksheets or reference books showing the proper form for footnotes should be available for students to study. This project uses *The Chicago Manual of Style* (see Reading Material for bibliographic information) as a standard footnote and bibliography reference.

Following the discussion students do a footnoting activity, as described on the assignment sheet. To prepare for this lesson, assemble a collection of periodicals and books and set up four or five "reference centers." There should be a common characteristic among all the books or periodicals in each center. For example, one center could be all encyclopedias, another could be all single-author books, a third could be two-author books, and a fourth could be three-or-more author books. A fifth center could be all periodicals. There could be a center that has books with no author, and one that has books assembled by editors or compilers. When these centers are ready, the Classroom Activity may begin.

On Your Own: After a class discussion about topic selection, each student chooses a topic and prepares a preliminary "working bibliography." This is done by locating at least ten sources of information about the chosen topic. These are recorded in proper bibliographic form on notecards, complete with page and (where appropriate) call numbers. A due date is set, and the working bibliographies are turned in on that day.

NOTE: If this assignment is leading directly to a term paper, students should take that into consideration before they choose their topics. When you discuss topic selection, emphasize that this assignment is a beginning step of a larger project; each student should decide on his or her topic, understanding that it will be the subject of a vigorous investigation, not just a quick look through some books and magazines. This could make a difference in what some people choose to study.

SUGGESTIONS FOR SETTING THE STAGE

- Ask colleagues, college professors, business people, and professionals to give you a one-paragraph explanation of why students should learn how to write a research paper. Read some of these to your class to help students see the value of such assignments. Establish in their minds that people in the real world use research and writing skills to make a living. They are important and valuable skills to have.

- Make a list of occupations, careers, undertakings, hobbies, avocations, and special situations that require research and the ability to write well-documented papers or reports. Present this list to the class and ask students to further expand it with ideas of their own. The point is that writing term papers is not a form of torture devised by uncaring teachers, but rather a way of preparing students to perform tasks that may be required of them in the future.

Name _____ Date _____

INTRODUCTORY NARRATIVE

Read the following narrative to see why Linda decided to teach herself how to write a research report.

Just the Facts, Please
by Linda

I've had plenty of teachers tell me that I'll have to do research projects some day, but I've never been faced with a requirement to write a properly constructed research paper. Of course, there have been several activities along the line where I had to find facts, record them on notecards, make bibliographies, write the information in my own words, and present what I'd learned to my classmates; but I've never had to prepare a formal report on a topic of my own choosing. When a reason to write one came along, I found myself at a loss as to how to begin and what to do.

I know that next semester Mr. Ortega is going to assign a research project and teach us about writing reports, but I needed to know this semester; I couldn't wait until March! A golden opportunity would have slipped away by then, and I didn't want that to happen. You see, I got a chance to be a guide and resource person in the city zoo's new primate house next summer. It's the *perfect* summer job. The Zoological Society sent a notice to all of the area high schools and colleges asking interested students to submit a formally written research paper about primates. Specific topics were left up to the applicants. The committee in charge of informational services will review the papers next month and select five students to whom summer jobs will be offered. The selections are to be announced soon after Christmas, followed by a ten-week series of Saturday morning workshops which the five students will attend. They will receive biology credit for this. The job begins with weekend work in May and extends to full time work in June.

Well, my research paper is finished, and I sent it today. I'm going to be nervous through Christmas vacation, wondering if I will be selected. I think I have a chance, because I wrote an informative and well-documented paper about orang-utans. The centerpiece of the primate house will be a group of orang-utans that the zoo is soon to acquire, so I figured that an in-depth knowledge of them would be desirable and even necessary for a qualified resource person. The committee will know after reading my paper that I know my orang-utans!

To prepare to write a research paper, I made an appointment to talk with Mr. Ortega after school one day. I asked him what I needed to know and how I could learn those things. He was very helpful. First, he warned me that writing a formal report is difficult. After convincing himself that I was serious and willing to do the work, he gave me some good advice (along with five reference books about writing reports, term papers, themes, theses, and dissertations). He told me to follow the "five *S*'s," which I have outlined below, as a way of systematically completing such a project. Using the reference books for technical guidance and the five *S*'s for organizational help, I wrote my paper in about six week's time. Now it's a waiting game, but I'm satisfied that I did a good job and that I've learned some valuable skills. That's something I'll always have, even if I don't get to work at the zoo.

© 1990 by The Center for Applied Research in Education

INTRODUCTORY NARRATIVE, CONT'D

Mr. Ortega's Five *S*'s

1. *Survey:* Topic selection is critical, so take your time and do it carefully. *Survey* means two things: (1) list and consider as many topics as possible before making a final choice; and (2) be certain there are plenty of reference materials available before proceeding. Encyclopedias and other general references are excellent places to begin a survey. This is also a good time to start preparing a working bibliography so you can keep track of what you have found.

2. *Specialize:* Choose one specific topic about which a research paper can be written. Do this only after a complete survey has been conducted. This topic becomes your *specialty*.

3. *Study:* Take time to *study* the topic before recording notes, making outlines, or in any way preparing the paper. As sources are located, record them as part of your working bibliography. During this study period (which may last a week or more) your main objective is to find out what is known about a topic and what kinds of information are available. This will help you decide what to emphasize in your report, which in turn will help in note taking.

4. *Summarize:* A big problem in writing a report is deciding what information to use and what to omit. Studying helps you decide; *summarizing* information on notecards allows you to record the facts you need so that they can be arranged and rearranged later. Try to avoid recording long quotes and entire paragraphs. *Summarize* the information you find in brief, useable statements of fact. This will help you write the report ''in your own words'' when it comes time to develop the actual text.

5. *Structure:* Get the *structuring* process started by grouping your notecards into general categories. These will become the major sections of the paper. Make an outline for the paper, listing the sections in the order you wish to present them. Then make the outline as detailed as possible by filling in important ideas that will be developed in each section. Organize your notecards according to the outline and check for any areas that need further research. Then write a rough draft. After proofreading (try to get other people to read the rough draft and comment on it), write a final draft, understanding that it too, might become a rough draft upon further proofreading. Remember to include footnotes and a complete bibliography.

Name _____ Date _____

READING MATERIAL

The books that Mr. Ortega gave Linda to use are listed in bibliographic form at the end of these notes. They are references that can be used by anyone embarking upon a research project. In one brief lesson it is impossible to fully cover all aspects of the research paper; for this reason you are directed to the reference books to find specific, detailed explanations of how to organize and write formal term papers.

A list of general considerations *is* possible, however, and that is what this lesson is about. Read the suggestions below to get an idea of what you should be able to do to successfully complete a research or term paper.

Before undertaking a research project, you should:

• Know how to select a good topic to study. Be especially careful to focus on something specific that can be fully covered in approximately ten typewritten (double-spaced) pages.

• Become proficient in the use of the library.

• Develop note-taking skills, especially the ability to record facts simply and succinctly.

• Devise a system for recording information on notecards.

• Understand how to group ideas and facts by organizing them into a detailed outline.

• Learn how to properly footnote a paper.

• Learn how to prepare a bibliography.

• Accept the fact that a rough draft is a necessity, and that a second draft may be needed as well.

• Know how to type.

• Resist the temptation to put things off until the last minute.

Bibliography

JAMES, ELIZABETH and BARKIN, CAROL. *How to Write a Term Paper*. New York: Lothrop, Lee, & Shepard Books, 1980.

LENMARK-ELLIS, BARBARA. *How to Write Themes and Term Papers*. 2d ed. New York: Barron's Educational Series, Inc., 1981.

The Chicago Manual of Style. 13th ed. Chicago: The University of Chicago Press, 1982.

MULKERNE, DONALD J.D. and MULKERNE, DONALD J.D. JR. *The Term Paper Step by Step*. 2d ed. Garden City, NY: Anchor Press/Doubleday, 1983.

TURABIAN, KATE L. *A Manual for Writers of Term Papers, Theses, and Dissertations*. 5th ed. Chicago: The University of Chicago Press, 1987.

These books may vary slightly in methods of organizing papers and preparing footnotes and bibliographies. Consistency is the key. Choose one acceptable method and use it throughout your paper.

Now read Linda's research paper. It should be noted that Linda used the widely accepted *Chicago Manual of Style* as her guide for footnotes and the bibliography at the end of her paper.

THE ORANG—UTANS OF BORNEO AND SUMATRA

by
Linda S. Blackburn

A RESEARCH PAPER

Zoological Society
Dr. Janice T. Goode

Richland Park Zoological Gardens
December 10, 19XX

TABLE OF CONTENTS

ORANG—UTAN: A STUDY OF THE RED APE

Orangutan is more correctly spelled orang—utan, meaning
''man of the jungle'' in the Malay language.[1] Until recently almost
nothing was known about orang—utans because they live in very dense
jungles and it was difficult to observe them in their treetop homes. Even
today little is known about many of their habits and social behaviors.[2]
Still, they are fascinating animals, and enough information is
available to make a fairly detailed study of them possible. Thanks to
the efforts of a few hardy and determined individuals who went into the
jungles of Borneo and Sumatra, we now have a basis for understanding how
orang—utans live their lives.

CLASSIFICATION

Orang—utans are a part of the animal kingdom, within the phylum
chordata (animals with a central nervous system), and subphylum
vertebrata (animals with backbones). They belong to the class
mammalia and are in the order primates, along with all other monkeys and
apes. Orang—utans share the family name simiidae with gorillas and
chimpanzees, but they have the genus name Pongo all to themselves. The
species name is pygmaeus, and so orang—utans are known scientifically
as Pongo pygmaeus.[3] Interestingly, the name ''Pongo'' comes
from the word ''impungo,'' which, in the early eighteenth century was
what the natives in Angola, Africa, called gorillas. British explorers
called gorillas Pongo, and somehow the word was then transferred to
orang—utans in later years.[4]

PHYSICAL APPEARANCE

Orang—utans are designed for traveling from branch to branch and
tree to tree in the highest levels of the jungle canopy. Their long,
curved fingers are perfectly adapted to grabbing and holding limbs, and
their extraordinary long arms allow them to swing across spaces of six
feet or even more. The thumb and big toe are located high up on the hand
and foot, which makes the long fingers and toes even more useful. Like a
thumb, the big toe is opposable to the other toes, which allows the foot
to be used for grasping.[5] The forelimbs (arms) are especially long from
the elbows on down to the hand, due to the elongation of two bones in the
lower arm: the radius and the ulna. By comparison, the legs are short
and have much less strength.[6]

The legs may appear awkward, but they are perfectly suited to
climbing and maneuvering in trees. The hip is constructed like a
shoulder, it has great mobility to move in arcs, unlike the hips of

other primates. This allows orang-utans to stretch, dangle, and contort in whatever way is necessary to grab the next branch. It also makes walking on the ground difficult. The combination of long arms, long fingers, long toes, short legs, and shoulder-like hips guarantees that the orang-utan will be most comfortable as a tree-dwelling animal.[7]

Two unique features of male orang-utans are the huge throat, or larynx sac, and the cheek flange. Fully developed males have massive folds of skin hanging from their necks which can be inflated with as much as six liters of air. These are used as resonators for their hollow, booming calls. Males can be heard ''pumping up'' their throat sacs as they prepare to make their call. Cheek flanges are broad pads of thick fat deposits which develop on the faces of males when they reach the age of twelve to fourteen years.[8] A mature male looks ''a lot like a big, saggily goitered, hairy, reddish Buddha wearing a baseball catcher's mask.''[9] Females also have throat sacs and face pads, but they are much less prominent.

Studies have revealed that males grow to about 4 feet 2 inches in height and females reach a height of 3 feet 6 inches. Males may have a fingertip to fingertip arm span of up to 7 feet 8 inches.[10] The weight of an adult male may reach an upper limit of 300 pounds, with the female being somewhat lighter.[11] In fact, it has been established that females are an average of 84 percent the size of males.[12] Orang-utans are very strong: a full-grown male is more than four times stronger than an adult man.[13] It is odd that an animal of such strength and size would live thirty to forty feet above the jungle floor, but orang-utans seem to manage it very well.

RANGE (Where Orang-Utans Can Be Found in the Wild)

Orang-utans are native to a very small portion of the Earth's surface, with a range of rain forest jungle that totals less than 50,000 square miles on the Malayan islands of Borneo and Sumatra. They inhabit three relatively small tracts of land in northwest Sumatra and five widely scattered territories in Borneo.[14] The equator runs directly through both islands, making the orang-utan's range truly tropical.

HABITAT

Orang-utans spend a good deal of their lives in trees, sleeping, eating, mating, and relaxing there. They do come to the ground, though, actually more often than was once believed. The equatorial rain forests are hot, steamy places, where plant growth is abundant most of the time.

Being primarily herbivores with a preference for fruit, orang-utans are nomadic as they search for ripe fruit and other vegetation. Each night they build nests in the crotches of tree branches high above the ground. These nests are abandoned daily. For a thorough description of the flora, fauna, climatic conditions, and geography of the orang-utan's habitat, see John MacKinnon's book, <u>In Search of the Red Ape</u>.[15]

LIFESTYLE/BEHAVIOR

The lifestyle and behavior of orang-utans is closely linked to food, which is a central concern of everyday life. Since fruit trees bear at different times of the year in a tropical rain forest, orang-utans are constantly moving around to follow their favorite foods. Because of their size and slow pace in the trees, an orang-utan can feed from only a small area each day, and a group or large family unit would not find enough to eat in such a small area. For this reason they prefer to travel singly or in small groups.[16] In fact, one of the most distinctive features of orang-utan life is its solitary nature. Adult males almost always live alone, and females are accompanied only by young offspring.[17]

Orang-utans are organized very loosely into larger groups under the domination of one large, older male. The group is usually not in visual contact with each other, but it remains united by the long, loud calls of the leader.[18] One of the services this old male provides is a detailed memory of where the choice fruit trees are located in the jungle and when each one bears its ripened fruit. As he visits the trees, his booming call alerts the members of his group to their location.[19] These calls are a series of groans that are said to sound ''like an old man in very great pain,'' and the roar can be heard for well over half a mile.[20]

Male orang-utans show aggression by terrific displays of branch-shaking, which causes a commotion; but when not confronting a rival, they are quite calm. Ironically, all of the macho showmanship also frightens the females, and it has been observed that the younger, less ferocious sub-adult males have more success courting and mating with females.[21]

The lifestyle and behavior of orang-utans has been affected by local human populations. Increasing numbers of people have brought about the wasteful use of slash-and-burn cultivation, which has forced orang-utans to live closer and closer together. Another threat to orang-utans in their natural habitat is poachers who illegally trade to private animal collectors and zoos that are willing to illegally obtain animals for their collections. A poacher usually kills a mother to get her baby, thereby eliminating two orang-utans from the wild.[22]

DIET

   The favorite foods of orang-utans are bubock and durian fruits and their sweet-tasting, nutty seeds. These fruits have prickly, tough shells that require strong hands and teeth to open. This is true of many of the fruits found in the tropical forest, and orang-utans are equipped with just such tools. When durian and bubock fruits are not available, the diet of orang-utans is amazingly varied. (See Table 1.) Many of these plants are unfamiliar, but each can be found in reference books which more fully describe them.[23] It should be remembered that some foods are favorites, some will do in a pinch, and some are only eaten when survival is at stake.

   The last item listed in Table 1 is interesting. Orang-utans visit certain mineral deposits on a regular basis and eat dirt by the handful. This gives them the mineral supplements they need, just as a salt lick provides minerals for deer or cows.[24]

TABLE 1

ORANG-UTAN DIET

Fruits from Malayan trees	Other foods
mata kuching	wadan (climbing bamboos)
bubock	lianas (climbing vines)
rambutans	orchids
lansats	wood pith
durian	insects
litchis	nuts
taraps	blossoms
mangoes	leaves
bananas	buds
wild plum	young shoots
figs	bark
	lizards
	tree frogs
	young birds
	other small animals
	mineral rich soil

Orang-utans are not tidy eaters. A large male will sit in the middle of a tree and pull branches to him, snapping them off in the process. When the fruit is all eaten, he leaves a wilted, broken tree. And, in times of plenty, orang-utans waste and destroy more than they eat by dropping partially eaten fruit to the ground.[25]

Surprisingly, there are seasons even in a tropical rain forest, and the fruit season is the period between April and November. During this season orang-utans ''stock up'' by feeding almost continuously. They have the ability to store up great quantities of fat in their bodies to serve as a reserve against leaner times. The cheek flanges described earlier are examples of fat storage by orang-utans. The ability to store fat is a curse to orang-utans in captivity, since they store it and don't burn it. This can cause them to become grotesquely overweight.[26]

AN ORANG-UTAN GROWS UP

The gestation period for orang-utans is about eight months, after which one baby (rarely two) is born. The newborn weighs from 1700 to 1900 grams (around 4 pounds) and is immediately able to grasp its mother's fur with its hands and feet. A baby orang-utan is almost totally helpless and will cling to its mother for loving attention and protection.[27] It may not be totally weaned from mother's milk for four years, during which time (especially the first two years) it is doted upon by an ever-present teacher who slowly introduces her child to the world.[28]

The baby is totally dependent on mother's milk for at least the first year. As it gets older it begins to sample fruits, but the transition to solid food is a long process. By age one, the young orang-utan is ready to begin exploring, and it ventures out on its own, testing its ability to climb. The baby rarely has a playmate its own age, since orang-utans are naturally solitary, so its mother is often its only companion. The second year sees more independence, along with further learning. The youngster learns how to gather fruit, how to build tree top nests, and how to construct ''umbrellas'' of leaves during a heavy rain. The third year brings a reduction in ties to the mother as she prepares to have another baby, she begins to reject her older child. By the fourth year a young male is on his own. His mother will have no more to do with him. A young female, however, will stay around her mother for several more years, during which time she prepares for parenthood by learning how to care for a baby brother or sister.[29]

Adolescent and sub-adult orang-utans do not travel with their parents. Much of their time is spent establishing their own ranges, learning their place in the social structure, and becoming involved in their first courtships. Females begin breeding at age seven and then have new infants every two to four years for most of their lives. Males continue to grow well into their teens, at which time the large face flanges, heavy jowls (throat sac), and long hair begin to develop. They begin calling at this time and become sexually active.[30]

Orang-utans may live until the age of forty or more,[31] and were it not for the hazards of the modern world, they could live their leisurely lives generation after generation in their own natural habitat. As it is, however, their territory is shrinking and their numbers are declining. They are registered as a species threatened with extinction. This is where zoos come in: to save the species, orang-utans should be bred in captivity, with the hope that some time it will be safe to put them back into the wild in Borneo and Sumatra.[32] Zoos play an important role in preserving endangered species. They provide a haven for animals that have been squeezed from their homes or hunted nearly to extinction, and they educate people about the plight of these animals. It now appears that zoos such as Richland Park Zoological Gardens are the orang-utan's only hope for survival.

FOOTNOTES

1. Barbara Harrison, <u>Orang-Utan</u> (Garden City, NY: Doubleday & Co., Inc., 1963), p. vii.

2. Jeffery H. Schwartz, <u>The Red Ape: Orang-Utans and Human Origins</u> (Boston: Houghton Mifflin Co., 1987), p. 2.

3. E. Laurence Palmer, <u>Fieldbook of Natural History</u> (New York: McGraw-Hill Book Co., 1949), p. 610.

4. Schwartz, <u>The Red Ape</u>, p. 17.

5. Erich Tylinek and Gotthard Berger, <u>Monkeys and Apes</u> (New York: Arco Publishing, Inc., 1985), p. 186.

6. Schwartz, <u>The Red Ape</u>, p. 5.

7. Ibid., pp. 6,7.

8. Tylinek, <u>Monkeys and Apes</u>, p. 186.

9. Schwartz, <u>The Red Ape</u>, p. 9.

10. Ibid., p. 10.

11. Prue Napier and John Napier, <u>Wild, Wild World of Animals: Monkeys and Apes</u> (Time-Life Films, Inc., 1976), p. 42.

12. Schwartz, <u>The Red Ape</u>, p. 10.

13. Ibid., p. 11.

14. Napier, <u>Wild, Wild World of Animals</u>, p. 42.

15. John MacKinnon, <u>In Search of The Red Ape</u> (New York: Holt, Rinehart and Winston, 1974), pp. 15-216.

16. Ibid., p. 59.

17. Ibid., p. 209.

18. Schwartz, <u>The Red Ape</u>, pp. 12-13.

19. Dan Freeman, <u>The Great Apes</u> (New York: G.P. Putnam's Sons, 1979), p. 60.

20. Napier, <u>Wild, Wild World of Animals</u>, p. 42.

21. MacKinnon, <u>In Search of The Red Ape</u>, p. 74.

22. Napier, <u>Wild Wild World of Animals</u>, p. 42; Tylinek, <u>Monkeys and Apes</u>, p. 189.

23. MacKinnon, <u>In Search of The Red Ape</u>, pp. 54, 62, 71, 119;
Schwartz, <u>The Red Ape</u>, p. 5; Napier, <u>Wild Wild World of Animals</u>, p. 42;
Tylinek, <u>Monkeys and Apes</u>, p. 186.

24. Schwartz, <u>The Red Ape</u>, p. 5.

25. MacKinnon, <u>In Search of The Red Ape</u>, p. 54; Schwartz,
<u>The Red Ape</u>, p. 10.

26. MacKinnon, <u>In Search of the Red Ape</u>, p. 119.

27. Tylinek, <u>Monkeys and Apes</u>, p. 187.

28. Napier, <u>Wild, Wild World of Animals</u>, p. 46.

29. Freeman, <u>The Great Apes</u>, pp. 64—66.

30. MacKinnon, <u>In Search of The Red Ape</u>, p. 181.

31. Freeman, <u>The Great Apes</u>, p. 62.

32. Tylinek, <u>Monkeys and Apes</u>, p. 190.

BIBLIOGRAPHY

Freeman, Dan. <u>The Great Apes</u>. New York: G.P. Putnam's Sons, 1979.

MacKinnon, John. <u>In Search of The Red Ape</u>. New York:
    Holt, Rinehart and Winston, 1974.

Napier, Prue and Napier, John. <u>Wild, Wild World of Animals: Monkeys and
    Apes</u>. Time—Life Films, Inc., 1976.

Schwartz, Jeffrey H. <u>The Red Ape: Orang—utans and Human
    Origins</u>. Boston: Houghton Mifflin Co., 1987.

Shuttlesworth, Dorothy E. <u>The Story of Monkeys, Great Apes, and Small
    Apes</u>. Garden City, NY: Doubleday & Co., Inc., 1972.

Tylinek, Erich and Berger, Gotthard. <u>Monkeys and Apes</u>. New York:
    Arco Publishing, Inc., 1985.

Name _____ Date _____

CLASSROOM ASSIGNMENT

Study the footnotes in Linda's report on orang-utans. Notice that the first time a source is cited, it is given a complete or full reference. Thereafter, it is referred to simply by the author's last name, the title (or a shortened version of the title), and the page number. Also notice that *ibid.* (*ibidem,* "in the same place") is used whenever the work being cited is the same as in the note immediately preceding it. A page number is always included.

Look at notes 22, 23, and 25. These are places in the report where closely associated information came from more than one source, or where two or more sources contain important information about a particular statement that has been made. Notes 7, 10, 13, 16, and 17 are examples of how *ibid.* is used, while 1, 2, 3, 5, 11, and 15 illustrate the proper form for full, or complete references. The remaining notes are written in short-title form. *The Chicago Manual of Style,* listed in the bibliography in the Reading Material, prefers the short-title form over the use of *"op. cit."* and *"loc. cit.,"* and this is the form that you are encouraged to use in your writing.

Now for some footnoting practice. Your teacher has placed books and magazines at several "reference centers" around the room. Follow this outline to complete the activity:

I. Choose a book or a magazine from one of the reference centers and take it to your desk.
    A. Locate a page that has factual information and write a two- or three-sentence summary or explanation of something you read there. Write this as if it were a part of a term paper. At the end of the last sentence indicate a footnote with a raised "1."
    B. On a separate piece of paper, record the footnote as a full reference, with complete information.
    C. Find another page in the same book or magazine, and repeat part "A," numbering your summary "2."
    D. On the footnote page, record note 2 using the short-title form. NOTE: you could use *ibid.* here, but the lesson is about full- and short-form notes, so follow the directions and don't use *ibid.*

II. Return the book or magazine to the reference center from which it came and then choose another one from a different center.
    A. Continue the same process by writing a brief statement based upon information from the second source, and number it "3."
    B. Record the note in full reference form on the footnote page.
    C. Write another brief statement based on information from a second page in this same book or magazine and number it "4."
    D. Record the note in short form on the footnote page.

III. Repeat this procedure until you have worked with at least one book or magazine from each reference center. For each source you will record two footnotes, one in full form and one in short form.

Name _____ Date _____

ON YOUR OWN

The proper way to begin a research paper is to develop a working bibliography, which is a collection of references to sources that have been discovered during preliminary research. Usually a working bibliography is made up of 3″ × 5″ notecards, each with a single reference recorded on it. Page numbers and library call numbers should be included so that when final research begins, information can be relocated quickly. The function of the working bibliography is to identify as many sources as possible before deciding which ones to actually use.

This lesson asks you to choose a topic (from within a subject area that your teacher has assigned) and begin to develop a working bibliography as if you were preparing to write a research paper. This may, in fact, be the first step of a formal research assignment for you. If so, your teacher will provide complete details about what to do once the working bibliography is finished.

To prepare a working bibliography, follow the outline below:

I. Come to the next class with five suggestions for topics that could be possible research projects from the subject area assigned by the teacher. Record them below. Be prepared to discuss your topic suggestions.

Subject area: _____

Topics: 1. _____

2. _____

3. _____

4. _____

5. _____

II. Choose a topic for this working bibliography assignment. The topic may come from the list above or from the class discussion.

My topic is: _____

III. Between now and the due date find at least ten sources of information about your chosen topic and record them in proper bibliographic form on notecards. Actually locate these sources at the library (or elsewhere) and find specific pages that have useful information. Be sure to record page numbers and call numbers on the bibliography cards.

IV. Investigate a variety of sources, such as textbooks, encyclopedias, reference books, magazines, almanacs, nonfiction books, and newspapers.

V. On the due date, hand in a working bibliography for the topic you have chosen.

Due Date _____